DINER

Barry Levinson

faber and faber

791.4372
~~LEV~~
LEV

First published in 1990 by Atlantic Monthly Press, USA
First published in Great Britain in 1991
by Faber and Faber Limited
3 Queen Square London WC1N 3AU

This edition published in 2000

Printed in England by Mackays of Chatham plc,
Chatham, Kent

A CIP record for this book is available from the British Library.

ISBN 0-571-20234-9

2 4 6 8 10 9 7 5 3 1

DINER

Fade in.

1. The screen

is black. We hear muffled rock and roll music. Then we read:

BALTIMORE
1959

Fade out.
Fade in.

2. Interior. Dance-hall basement. Night.

FENWICK *walks along the dimly lighted basement. Heavy winter coats hang from hooks on the wall. In the background there is constant traffic of people entering and leaving the rest rooms. From above we hear the muffled sound of the rock-and-roll* BAND.

FENWICK *is in his early twenties and is dressed in the Joe College style of the late fifties—sports jacket, button-down shirt, chino pants, and Bass Weejuns. We sense that he is a little lost in himself, confused. He looks out one of the windows onto the parking lot. Then, without any outward anger, he punches his fist through a windowpane. Seconds later he breaks another window with his fist.*

FENWICK, *picking up the beat of the music from above, struts to the sound as he approaches another bank of windows. He calmly breaks another windowpane with his fist.*

A GUY *coming out of the bathroom in the background sees* FENWICK's *actions and then heads up the steps.*

Cut to

3. Interior. Dance hall.

The crowd is gathered around the bandstand, listening to the local group, THE SHAKERS,

*playing their popular hit "Hot Nuts." The song is played toward the end of the evening
because of its risqué lyrics.*

> BAND LEADER
>
> Hot nuts, hot nuts, get from the peanut man.
> Hot nuts, hot nuts, get 'em any way you can.

As the crowd swings the verse back to the BAND LEADER, *the* GUY *who spotted* FENWICK
breaking the windows approaches BOOGIE. BOOGIE *is something of a dandy, flashier in dress
than others in his crowd. Although he isn't particularly good looking, something about his
attitude is very appealing to girls.* BOOGIE, *after listening to the* GUY, *heads downstairs.*

4. Interior. Dance-hall basement.

FENWICK *casually breaks another window with his fist. His hand is bleeding.* BOOGIE
approaches.

> BOOGIE
>
> What's up, Fen?

> FENWICK
>
> Just breaking windows, Boog.

> BOOGIE
>
> What for?

> FENWICK
>
> It's a smile.

He breaks another window with his fist.

> BOOGIE
>
> C'mon, don't be a schmuck.

> FENWICK
>
> I know that glass is made from sand, but how come you can see
> through it?

He breaks another window. BOOGIE *grabs him.*

> BOOGIE
>
> Leave the windows alone. What's the matter with you?

> FENWICK
>
> It's a smile, that's all.

> BOOGIE
>
> I'm cracking up.

FENWICK *struggles to get free.*

BOOGIE (*continuing*)

I'm warning you, Fen, break another window and you're gonna get a fat lip.

He lets FENWICK *go.*

BOOGIE (*continuing*)

Where's your date?

FENWICK

Gave her away.

BOOGIE

What?

FENWICK

Gave her away. David Frazer said she was death. So I said if you like the way she looks, take her.

BOOGIE

What are you, the Salvation Army?

FENWICK

Charged him five bucks.

BOOGIE

C'mon. Upstairs.

FENWICK *just stares at him.*

BOOGIE (*continuing*)

C'mon.

They walk away from the camera.

BOOGIE (*continuing*)

You really are nuts, you know that?

FENWICK

Me? What about her? She didn't have to go. I'm nuts. Get that.

BOOGIE

That's what you get from dating eleventh-graders. Brains aren't developed.

FENWICK

But her tits were.

BOOGIE

Falsies.

FENWICK

They were?

BOOGIE

Firsthand info.

FENWICK

Shit, then what am I pissed about?

They disappear up the steps.

Cut to

5. Interior. Dance hall. Slightly later.

The BAND *is on a break. A Frank Sinatra record is playing. The camera pans to* EDDIE, *who is in a corner with one foot up on a chair. He smokes a cigarette and taps his foot lightly to the music.* EDDIE *takes Sinatra very seriously.*

SHREVIE *approaches* EDDIE.

SHREVIE

Where's Elyse?

EDDIE

Talking with your wife about the fucking wedding plans.

SHREVIE

Gettin' cold feet?

EDDIE

They've never been warm.

BOOGIE *is talking with* DIANE, *the young eleventh-grader whom* FENWICK *had the falling-out with. She is an attractive, petite girl with large breasts.*

BOOGIE

How can you take Frazer over the Fen?

DIANE

'Cause.

BOOGIE

Diane, did you know that Frazer bought you for five bucks?
That's the kinda guy he is.

DIANE

He did?

BOOGIE

Do you want to leave with Frazer?

DIANE

Not really, but Fenwick scares me. Why don't you take me
home?

>   BOOGIE
> Diane, I'm in law school at night. I have to go home and study.
> I just stopped by here 'cause I appreciate fine music.
>
>   DIANE
> I thought you worked in a beauty parlor.
>
>   BOOGIE
> I do during the day.

He puts his hand up and strokes her cheek. In the background we can see FRAZER *standing with another guy. He glances over.*

>   BOOGIE (*continuing*)
> Diane, go with Fen. For me, OK?

Cut to

6. Exterior. Country road. Night.

FENWICK's *TR3 speeds by.* DIANE *is in the car.* FENWICK *is telling her something, and she laughs.*

7. Interior. Fenwick's car. Night.

>   FENWICK
> You cold?
>
>   DIANE
> No.
>
>   FENWICK
> I didn't turn the heater on.

7A. Exterior. Country road. Night.

BOOGIE *and* MODELL *follow. Behind them* SHREVIE *and his wife,* BETH, *follow in a 1950 Hudson Hornet.*

FENWICK *floors his car and disappears around a bend. The other cars do not keep pace.*

8. Interior. Boogie's car.

>   MODELL
> You know what word I'm not comfortable with? *Nuance.* It's not
> really a word like *gesture. Gesture* is a good word. At least you

know where you stand with *gesture*. . . . But *nuance,* I don't know.
. . . Maybe I'm wrong.

9. Interior. Shrevie's car.

BETH

Elyse feels that Eddie is getting very sensitive about the wedding.

SHREVIE

I know. We were talking about it.

10. Interior. Fenwick's car.

DIANE

Aren't you chilly?

FENWICK

No, no . . . I feel good. . . . I feel good.

(*a beat*)

Am I going too fast for you?

DIANE

No, no.

11. Interior. Shrevie's car.

BETH

Elyse's mother is very upset with Eddie. They picked out a
yellow and white motif for the wedding. You know, like we
did—tablecloth, napkins, maids of honor. Anyway, Eddie ob-
jected. He wanted blue and white because that's the Colts'
colors. Refused to give in.

SHREVIE

Yeah, so?

BETH

Well, you know how stubborn Eddie is.

SHREVIE

Could be worse. It could be black and gold. Steelers' colors.

SHREVIE *notices* BOOGIE's *taillights come on. He slows down. Something is wrong up ahead.*

12. Exterior. Roadside. Night.

FENWICK's *car is turned over. The headlights shine brightly against a tree.*

It's difficult to see exactly what has happened in the darkness. BOOGIE *and* MODELL, SHREVIE *and* BETH *exit their respective cars and walk toward the accident.*

As they approach, we see FENWICK *lying halfway out of the car covered in blood.* DIANE *cannot be seen.*

SHREVIE (*to* BETH)

Stay here.

The three guys move apprehensively toward the car. FENWICK's *face is covered in blood, so much so that it can hardly be recognized.*

MODELL *reacts to the sight of* FENWICK's *face.*

MODELL

Oh Jesus.

BOOGIE *kneels next to* FENWICK. *After a beat* FENWICK *explodes with laughter.*

BOOGIE

You son of a bitch!

FENWICK *screams with laughter.*

BOOGIE (*continuing*)

You asshole!

Then BOOGIE *laughs. The rest of the* GUYS *join in. Not* BETH. *She is not amused.* FENWICK *crawls out of the Triumph.*

FENWICK

I really got you guys, didn't I? Didn't I? Been carrying a ketchup bottle around for weeks.

DIANE *steps out of the woods. She laughs nervously.*

DIANE

I hid in the woods. Didn't want any ketchup on me.

FENWICK

Weeks. Just lookin' for the right time.

MODELL

You got me. Christ, I thought you bought it.

FENWICK

Real hard holding back the laughs. *Real* hard.

BOOGIE

You outdid yourself.

                                    BETH
That's very mature, Fenwick.

                                    FENWICK
Fuck mature.

                                    SHREVIE
Hey!

                                    FENWICK
Sorry, Beth.

                                    BOOGIE
Turned the car over yourself?

                                    FENWICK
Yeah. Give me a hand.

                                    BOOGIE
No way.

                                    FENWICK
C'mon.

BOOGIE *starts back to his car. The others follow.*

FENWICK *pleads with them.* BOOGIE, *with his back to* FENWICK, *is amused, delighted that he's got* FENWICK *on a number.*

                          BOOGIE (*with the authority of a schoolteacher*)
Fenwick, you turned that car over. You must put it upright
yourself. You need some discipline in your life.

                                    FENWICK
C'mon, guys. It was easy pushing it over 'cause of the angle. It'll
be a bitch getting it up.

BOOGIE *and* MODELL *get into* BOOGIE's *car.* SHREVIE *and* BETH *get into the Hudson.*

                                    MODELL
Have you tried? You haven't tried.

                             FENWICK (*desperate*)
I'm buying at the diner.

Without missing a beat, BOOGIE *and* MODELL *exit the car.*

                                    BOOGIE
Schmuck, another five seconds and you'd've had us for free.

They laugh. SHREVIE *starts his car.*

13. Interior. Shrevie's car. Night.

BETH

You guys really are sick, you know that?

SHREVIE

That's 'cause you got no sense of humor.

He pulls away from the side of the road.

SHREVIE *(continuing; yelling out the window)*

See you guys later at the diner.

Cut to

14. Exterior. Diner. Night.

The diner is a typical late-forties metal and glass structure, almost deco in design. Cars are parked in front, including SHREVIE'S *Hudson Hornet. The camera pans to a car parked over in a corner.*

TABACK *has his trunk open. It is filled with pants. A few guys, including* FRAZER, *are going through the goods as* TABACK *tries to wheel and deal.*

TABACK *(to* FRAZER*)*

Seven bucks. All wool. You can't beat it.

FRAZER *(holding them up)*

The crotch looks too short. Don't care for that.

TABACK

What are you afraid it's gonna get caught in the crack between your legs?

The other GUYS *"Whooo" in reaction to* TABACK'S *put-down.*

FRAZER

You sure are hot shit since you've taken over your father's business here.

He throws the pants back and walks away.

Cut to

15. Interior. Diner. Night.

The diner is the *late-night hangout. It attracts a mixed-bag crowd.*

Around one side are the aluminum-siding salesmen—guys in their thirties and forties. There are some HIGH-SCHOOLERS, *only there on the weekends, and the* BOOGIE-SHREVIE *crowd—the guys in their early twenties. One thing is quite apparent: there are no girls present, except the* WAITRESSES. *That is the unspoken rule—*no dates.

EDDIE, SHREVIE, *and* MODELL *sit in a booth. They eat french fries and gravy.*

EDDIE

You can't compare Mathis to Sinatra. No way.SHREVIE
They're both great singers.

EDDIE

Yeah, but you can't compare them. Sinatra is the lord. He's big in movies, everything.

SHREVIE

If Mathis wasn't a blue, he'd be a big movie star.

MODELL

That's true. There's hardly any blues in movies. Just sidekicks.

EDDIE

C'mon, they could've put Mathis in *From Here to Eternity*. They had blues in the war.

SHREVIE

Mathis didn't come around until after that movie.

EDDIE

Are you telling me Mathis could've played Maggio? Is that what I'm hearing?

MODELL

Who do you make out to? Sinatra or Mathis?

EDDIE

For that, Mathis.

SHREVIE

I'm married. We don't make out.

They laugh.

FENWICK *enters and approaches* GEORGE, *the manager, at the cashier area.*

FENWICK

George, you got a Band-Aid?

FRAZER *wanders by.*

FRAZER

Sorry about the Diane thing. I didn't know you, uh, had a thing for her.

FENWICK

Yeah, yeah. . . . It's OK; it's OK.

GEORGE

What'd you do, cut your hand?

FENWICK

Yeah, yeah . . . I don't know *what* happened.

FRAZER

What about my five bucks?

FENWICK

Gimme a couple of days.

Then FENWICK *heads toward the* GUYS *and passes the* WAITRESS.

FENWICK

Enid, french fries and gravy, and a cherry Coke.

He sits down and joins the GUYS.

SHREVIE

How'd it go?

FENWICK

Pretty good. Said she never wanted to see me again.

MODELL

Charmed her, huh?

FENWICK

All I did was park the car on a nice, lonely road. I looked at her
and said, "Fuck or fight."

SHREVIE

Hey, that's a good line. . . . I'm gonna use that myself sometime.

MODELL

You always know the right thing to say.

SHREVIE

How old is she?

EDDIE

She's jailbait.

SHREVIE

What is she, twelve?

MODELL

She'll be twelve.

They all laugh.

SHREVIE

She'll be twelve.

FENWICK

She's old enough to know better. No, . . . I'm kidding.

16. Interior. Diner.

Angle on the WAITRESS *coming out of the kitchen*

ENID (*yelling to* GEORGE)

George, will you come here and talk to him. . . . He's driving
me wild.

GEORGE *goes toward the kitchen, opens the door, and yells in Greek.*

17. Interior. Diner.

Angle on the GUYS *in the booth*

MODELL (*to* EDDIE)

What's that, roast beef?

EDDIE

Don't ask me this anymore, Modell. Yes.

MODELL

Gonna finish that?

EDDIE

Yeah, I'm gonna finish it. I paid for it; I'm not going to give it
to you.

MODELL

Because if you're not gonna finish it, I would eat it, . . . but if
you're gonna eat it—

EDDIE

What do you want?! Say the words.

MODELL

No, . . . if you're gonna eat it, you eat; that's all right.

EDDIE

Say the words: "I want the roast-beef sandwich." Say the
words, and I'll give you a piece.

SHREVIE

Will you cut this out. I mean, every time!

EDDIE

He doesn't talk.

SHREVIE

But you know what he means, right?

EDDIE

Yeah, I know what he means, . . . but he beats about the bush.
. . . He beats about the bush. If he said the words, I'd give him
a piece.

MODELL

If I wanted it, wouldn't I ask?

EDDIE

Then ask. You know you want it.

SHREVIE

Will you let it go!

MODELL

You're an annoying asshole.

EDDIE

I'm annoying? I'm trying to eat a meal by myself.

SHREVIE

If you want to give him the sandwich, give him the sandwich.
If you don't want to give him the sandwich, don't.

EDDIE

I don't want to. . . . Look at his eyes.

MODELL

I asked one, simple question. . . . You know, the trouble with
you, you don't chew your food. . . . That's why you get so
irritable. You've got lumps. . . . you've got like roast beef that
just stays there.

EDDIE

Modell! Now you're really, really getting me mad. Now my
blood is boiling.

SHREVIE

I'll take the sandwich.

He leans over to EDDIE's *plate and picks up the roast-beef sandwich.*

EDDIE

You see. . . . You do this every time.

MODELL

Why are you blaming me? He took your sandwich. I'm sitting here having a cup of coffee. . . .

SHREVIE (*to* EDDIE)

You want this? You want this?

EDDIE (*getting madder*)

No, no!

FENWICK

I do.

EDDIE

I can't believe this. You two play against me; that's what the problem is. You're on each other's sides.

18. Interior. Diner.

Angle on BOOGIE *talking to* GEORGE *at the till*

BOOGIE

Come on, George.

GEORGE

You owe me ten dollars already.

BOOGIE

Don't be like that.

GEORGE

I don't want to talk to you.

19. Interior. Diner—the aluminum-siding guys' booth

Angle on BAGEL *holding court with his* GUYS.

BAGEL (*calling over to* BOOGIE)

Boog, come here.

BOOGIE *approaches.*

BAGEL (*continuing*)

You lay down a bet with Barnett?

BOOGIE

Don't remember.

BAGEL

C'mon, nobody bets two thousand and forgets.

BOOGIE

OK, so? What's the point, Bagel?

BAGEL

Where you getting two thousand? You haven't got a pot to piss in.

BOOGIE

Game's a lock.

BAGEL

Nothing's a lock. You want me to call it off? As a favor to your father, may he rest in peace.

BOOGIE

Leave my father out of it.

BOOGIE *walks off.*

BAGEL

Kids today. Nobody's interested in making an honest buck.

CARSON

Heard he wants to be a lawyer.

BAGEL

That's what I'm saying. You call that an honest buck?

BOOGIE *approaches the* GUYS *and sits down.*

BOOGIE

Bagel heard about my basketball bet.

MODELL

I'm down for fifty.

BOOGIE

Woo, big spender. I'm telling you. They're shaving points on the game. This is no bullshit tip. Get in, guys.

MODELL

You heard they're shaving points?

EDDIE

How do you know?

SHREVIE

I heard about your bets before. . . . It cost me fifty bucks.

EDDIE

What's your resource?

SHREVIE

Don't get in.

BOOGIE

Come on, they're shaving points on this game. You want in or what?

MODELL

They're definitely shaving points? You feel secure? Who's the guy?

BOOGIE

Why do you have to ask so many questions.

MODELL

Because I don't know who the guy is. Do you trust him? . . . Make it fifteen. . . . Make it fifteen. No, make it twenty.

SHREVIE

Don't do it, Modell. I mean, I lost fifty bucks on the last game.

EDDIE (*to* BOOGIE)

Let me ask you a question.

MODELL

Oh no.

EDDIE

Will you be quiet.

(*to* BOOGIE)

Listen, who do you pick? Sinatra or Mathis?

SHREVIE

Would you just let this die?

EDDIE

It's important to me.

SHREVIE

It's annoying to me, OK. You've been asking that question to every Mo that walks in here. Will you just forget it.

EDDIE

Maybe I've got something to gain from the answer, OK.

SHREVIE

It doesn't matter.

EDDIE

Let the man speak.

BOOGIE

Presley.

SHREVIE

There you go . . . the definitive answer. . . . It's Presley?

MODELL

It's Presley?

EDDIE

You're sick. You've gone two steps below in my book now. . . .

SHREVIE

Did you learn something from that?

20. Interior. Diner. Later.

The GUYS *are still hanging out at the diner.*

BOOGIE

Did I tell you guys I'm taking out Carol Heathrow tomorrow
night?

FENWICK

You're taking out Carol Heathrow?

BOOGIE (*sarcastically*)

No, *you're* taking her out.

EDDIE

She is death.

BOOGIE

Only go for the best.

SHREVIE

Cold.

MODELL

She's not a smart girl. Did you ever talk to her?

BOOGIE

What's the bet she goes for my pecker on the first date?

FENWICK

The only hand on your schlong is gonna be yours.

BOOGIE

Bet me twenty.

FENWICK

You got it.

EDDIE

I'm in.

MODELL

Me too.

SHREVIE

I'm in, but we need validation.

BOOGIE

All right. I'll arrange it.

SHREVIE

How? What you gonna do, get fingerprints? I tell you, I'm not
gonna do the testing.

They all laugh.

21. Exterior. Diner. Night.

EDDIE *and* MODELL *button up their coats against the cold as they leave the diner.*

MODELL

You bring your car?

EDDIE

No, I walked! Yeah, I brought my car.

MODELL

You going straight home, or you—

EDDIE

No, I'm going by way of Atlantic City! What kind of question
is that?

MODELL

I'll wait for the other guys.

EDDIE

You constantly do this. You constantly walk out behind me.
. . . You stand there. . . .

MODELL

Maybe you've got plans or something.

EDDIE

No, I don't have plans. It's four in the morning. I have no plans.
You want a ride?

MODELL

I'll go with you if you want. You want me to—

EDDIE

Say the words: "I want a ride."

MODELL

I don't have to go home.

EDDIE

I enjoy your company. You want a ride?

MODELL

I'll go with you, sure.

EDDIE

You got gas money? Just kidding. You're so serious lately, Modell.

Cut to

22. Interior. B & O railroad station. Night.

The GUYS *mill around the platform as* PASSENGERS *leave a train that has just arrived and
walk toward the camera.*

BILLY HALPERT *steps off the train.* BILLY *is in his early twenties and wears the typical
button-down shirt, crew-neck sweater, chino pants, and Bass Weejuns. He sees the* GUYS.

BILLY

You guys are too much. How'd you know I was comin' in this
morning?

BOOGIE

We know . . . we know everything.

SHREVIE

You up for some diner?

BILLY (*smiling*)

What do you think?

They start to pass the kiosk area in the center of the terminal.

FENWICK

Hold on a second. I'm gettin' some coffee here.

SHREVIE

Coffee? You have to have coffee before we go to the diner to have coffee?

BILLY (*to* BOOGIE)

I can't believe Eddie's gettin' married. I can't believe it!

BOOGIE

He's crazy is what he is. With the Shrevie here it was just nuts, but Eddie? That's lunacy.

SHREVIE

Marriage is all right. I'm not complaining.

BOOGIE

Not complaining. Ummm, sounds good.

FENWICK

'Course it isn't a hundred percent sure yet.

(*to* MAN *behind the counter*)

You got some cream?

BILLY

What? He's getting married on New Year's Eve.

BOOGIE

Not until she takes the test.

BILLY

Boog, what are you talking about?

FENWICK

Eddie's going to give Elyse a football test. If she fails, the marriage is off.

(*to* SHREVIE)

You got a nickel? I don't wanna break a five.

BILLY

What are you guys puttin' me on? This a joke or somethin'?

BOOGIE

You know Eddie and the Colts. Very serious. The test has something like a hundred and forty questions. True and false, multiple choice, short answer.

They start to walk away from the kiosk.

FENWICK

Oral test. He doesn't want any cheating.

BILLY

What happens if she fails? He's going to call it off? Is that what
I hear?

SHREVIE

He swears to it. The test was supposed to be two months ago.
Elyse keeps delaying. Heavy pressure.

Cut to

23. Exterior. B & O railroad station. Night.

The GUYS *walk across the parking lot toward* SHREVIE's *car. The parking lot is relatively
quiet, save for a half-dozen cars and a few taxicabs.*

FENWICK

Her plan could be, though, to stall until the last minute. Then
if she fails, it doesn't matter. It's a *fait accompli.* Knot's tied.

BOOGIE

Fait accompli my ass. He walks.

BILLY

I doubt it. I tell you, it was a real surprise. No call. Just a note.
Why do you figure, all of a sudden?

BOOGIE

Bottom line? Elyse turns into Iceland and Eddie's not the type
to look elsewhere. Eddie goes for the marriage, and Elyse is back
to being the Bahamas again.

They get into the Hudson.

SHREVIE

You don't know that for sure, Boog.

BOOGIE

I'm a good judge of human nature.

*The Hudson starts to pull away. It moves down the parking lot away from the camera.
As it turns at the corner, it disappears from sight.*

Cut to

24. Exterior. Street. Daybreak.

The Hudson heads down a brick street and drives away from the camera.

Cut to

25–29. Exterior. Montage. Daybreak.

Five city scenes in the quiet, early morning
Cut to

30. Exterior. Harbor. Daybreak.

The sun is breaking over the water, the factory smokestacks billowing with white smoke.
The Hudson drives by.

31. Exterior. Diner. Day.

The Hudson is parked out front. The morning light is just beginning to break. Through
the windows we can see the GUYS *sitting in a booth eating. They are obviously having a*
good time. SHREVIE *takes a sip of coffee.* BILLY *says something, and* SHREVIE *puts his hand*
to his mouth. Coffee pours through his fingers and down his chin.
Cut to

32. Interior. Diner. Day.

BILLY

And that was nothing compared to what happened in Miss
Nathan's class.

SHREVIE

This is great. I was there.

BILLY

Had her for art class. Third floor. She catches me talking. Tells
me to see her after class. I jumped up from my seat and started
screaming, "I can't take it any more! You're always picking on
me! I can't stand it!" Then I ran to the window, opened it, and
jumped out. She freaks and faints dead away. She forgot the
gym roof was six feet below.

SHREVIE

Her eyes closed. She swayed for a moment and then toppled
right over her high heels. Out cold. I was hysterical.

BILLY

The topper was the principal. Donley comes in and sees Miss
Nathan on the floor. He doesn't know what to make of it.

SHREVIE

Then Sherman, remember him? Normally a schmuck, but he stands up and says, "Shhhhhh, she's sleeping, Mr. Donley." Then he sees Billy in the window.

BILLY

I said, "I'm sorry I'm late, sir, but my bus broke down. Is Miss Nathan up yet?"

All the GUYS *laugh.*

BOOGIE

You're missing the action now, Billy. Half the guys are at U of B night school. A lot of fucking laughs.

FENWICK (*to* BILLY)

A masters in business. That's the lowest.

BILLY *shrugs his shoulders as if to say, "What can I tell you?"*

BILLY

Who's there?

BOOGIE

Eddie, of course. Burton.

BILLY

Burton?

BOOGIE

Dropped out of rabbinical school. Henry . . .

FENWICK

Cliff, the Mouse . . .

SHREVIE

Youssel.

BOOGIE

Thrown out.

SHREVIE

Yeah?

BOOGIE

Accidentally stole some money from one of the teachers.

BILLY

U of B's busy at night, huh?

BOOGIE

And then there's me.

BILLY

Yeah? You at law school?

BOOGIE

Thought I'd take a pop with the law. Although I'm still working
the beauty salon.

Cut to

33. Exterior. Residential neighborhood. Day.

*The Hudson slowly moves down the quiet, tree-lined street. All is quiet, the morning having
yet to begin. The neighborhood is well cared for—a pleasant, middle-class area. The car
pulls up in front of a three-story, white shingled house.* BILLY *exits the car with his suitcase.*

BILLY

See you guys at the diner tonight.

He slams the door shut. The car pulls away. BILLY *walks up the steps, pulls out a key,
and opens the door.*

Cut to

34. Interior. Halperts' house. Day.

BILLY *walks up the steps to the second floor. He sees that his* PARENTS' *door is open and
peeks inside. The bed is made. No one is there. He turns toward his* SISTER's *room. The
camera pans. The bed is also made. He goes up the stairs to the third floor.*

35. Interior. Halperts' house.

Angle on a black door

A sign reads NO ADMITTANCE. BILLY *enters.*

Cut to

36. Interior. Billy's room.

BILLY *lies on the bed in his shorts, smoking a cigarette. The camera slowly pans the room.
An upright piano is in a corner. Then we see magazine pictures of various baseball stars
tacked on the wall. The camera pans to pennants of the Baltimore Orioles and the Baltimore
Colts. The camera drifts over to* Playboy *centerfolds. Then we see a photograph of* BILLY
and a bunch of the GUYS *leaning against a railing in Atlantic City during their high-school
years.*

Cut to

37. Exterior. Halperts' house. Day.

BILLY *walks away from his house, crosses the street, and climbs the steps of another house. He rings the doorbell.*

Seconds later the door opens. MRS. SIMMONS, *a short, heavyset woman, stands there.*

> MRS. SIMMONS (*pleased*)
> Billy, you're in town already?

> BILLY
> Yeah, thought I'd spend the holidays here. Lot of parties, I hear.

He enters.

38. Interior. Simmons' house. Day.

BILLY *and* MRS. SIMMONS *walk down the hallway. In the background* CLEANING LADY *is vacuuming.*

> MRS. SIMMONS
> Did you know your parents are out of town?

> BILLY
> No.

> MRS. SIMMONS
> They're in Florida. Be back for Eddie's wedding, though.

> BILLY
> He still sleeping?

> MRS. SIMMONS
> What else? It's only two thirty. Wake him.

BILLY *starts up the steps.*

> MRS. SIMMONS (*continuing*)
> I'll be happy when he's out of the house.

Cut to

39. Interior. Eddie's room.

It is a total mess. Clothes, underwear, and shoes are strewn all over the room. BILLY *shakes* EDDIE. *His eyes open.*

> EDDIE
> Whaddya say, Bill?

> BILLY
> Still the early riser, huh?

EDDIE *reaches over to the night table and lights a Pall Mall.*

EDDIE
Nothin' changes.

BILLY
Except you getting married.

EDDIE
Yeah, ain't that a kick.

He gets out of bed, picks up a pair of pants from the floor, and steps into them.

EDDIE (*continuing*)
Thought you weren't coming in until New Year's Eve.

BILLY
Nothing's happening around campus, so . . .

EDDIE *puts on a shirt and a tie with an already-made knot. He pulls the tie up and then starts buttoning the rest of the shirt.*

EDDIE
You bring in that girl with you?

BILLY
Broke up.

EDDIE
Shame. In that picture you sent, looked like she had great knockers.

BILLY
Yeah.

(*a beat*)
Didn't figure on you and Elyse so soon.

EDDIE *searches the floor and picks out two socks that are similar but not the same.*

EDDIE
I figured New Year's Eve would be good. Get married. Party through the night. You know.

He puts the socks on. They have holes in the heels.

BILLY
I was pissed off, Ed. Figured you would call or something. Let me know you were planning it.

EDDIE
Yeah, I know. But you're my best man.

BILLY

What do you think? Of course I'm your best man.

Eddie walks into the bathroom. The camera follows. He splashes some water on his face and wipes it with a wash rag.

BILLY

Boogie and the guys picked me up at the train station.

EDDIE *takes a drag on his cigarette and puts it on the toilet seat. Then he squirts some toothpaste onto the toothbrush.*

EDDIE *(with a mouth full of toothpaste)*

Yeah? I left the diner at five. They didn't say anything to me.

BILLY

Surprise, I guess.

EDDIE

How'd they know?

BILLY

Barbara Kohler told Fenwick.

EDDIE

You keep in touch, huh?

BILLY

Yeah.

EDDIE

You're still nailing her, aren't you, you son of a bitch.

EDDIE *spits the toothpaste out and sticks his mouth under the faucet to rinse, making sure to keep his tie dry.*

BILLY

Never did.

EDDIE *wipes his mouth with his hand.*

EDDIE

Who you kidding?

He puts the cigarette back in his mouth and starts out of the room. BILLY *follows.*

EDDIE *(continuing)*

What else would you be doing with her all these years?

BILLY

Talking.

40. Interior. Simmons' house.

Another angle as they start down the stairs

> EDDIE
>
> Talking? Shit, if you want to talk, there's always the guys at the diner. You don't need a girl if you want to talk.

> BILLY
>
> Eddie, you'll never change.

> EDDIE
>
> Damn right.

Cut to

41. Interior. Simmons' kitchen.

MRS. SIMMONS *is on the telephone as* EDDIE *and* BILLY *enter.*

> MRS. SIMMONS
>
> I saw it. It was in the papers this morning, Marion. . . . Yes, this morning.

> EDDIE (*to* BILLY)
>
> You and I'll shoot some pool.

> BILLY
>
> Haven't shot pool in ages.

> EDDIE
>
> Well, it's about time; otherwise you'll lose your edge.

> MRS. SIMMONS
>
> You still have the morning paper, Marion?

> EDDIE
>
> Ma, what's for breakfast?

> MRS. SIMMONS
>
> The kitchen is closed.

EDDIE *sits down at the table.* BILLY *sits down on a chair over by the wall.*

> EDDIE
>
> I'm hungry here.

> MRS. SIMMONS
>
> Hold on, Marion.

(*to* EDDIE)

You want something to eat? Make it. I haven't got all day to wait on you.

EDDIE

Come on, Ma. Don't give me that shit. A fried bologna sandwich will be good.

MRS. SIMMONS (*turning around angrily*)

Get out of the house! Billy, take him out of here!

EDDIE

A fried bologna sandwich is not a lot to ask for, for Christsake!

MRS. SIMMONS

Just a second, Marion.

MRS. SIMMONS *puts down the receiver, picks up a butcher knife from the counter by the sink, and waves it at* EDDIE.

MRS. SIMMONS

Eddie, you're giving me a headache! Take a walk.

EDDIE *rises from his chair.*

EDDIE

You want to stab me? Come on! Come on!

He brings up his fist and assumes a boxing position. MRS. SIMMONS *moves toward* EDDIE *wielding the knife.* EDDIE *backs around the table.* BILLY *watches this scene without expression.*

MRS. SIMMONS

You miserable creature.

EDDIE

Take your best shot. Then I'm going to punch your lights out, Ma.

MRS. SIMMONS (*stalking him*)

Who do you think you are!

EDDIE

Come on! Come on! Go for the cut; then you're down and out.

The short, heavyset woman continues to stalk EDDIE *as they move around the table.* BILLY *is not disturbed or surprised. This is apparently an ongoing occurrence.*

MRS. SIMMONS

How did you turn into such a thing!

EDDIE

I've got fists of granite. You're going down.

MRS. SIMMONS (*turning away*)

I'm not going to ruin a good knife on you. It's not worth it.

EDDIE *turns to* BILLY *and smiles.*

BILLY (*quietly*)

So what's new?

MRS. SIMMONS (*opening the refrigerator*)

Eat a sandwich, then give me some peace. Billy, you want something?

BILLY

No, thanks.

MRS. SIMMONS

You sure? It's no trouble.

BILLY

No, really.

MRS. SIMMONS (*picking up the telephone receiver*)

Marion, lemme call you back. I'm gonna fix the kids some breakfast.

Cut to

42. Interior. Appliance store. Day.

*Tight shot—TV screen—*Little Women, *an old feature film, is on the set.*

CUSTOMER (*offscreen*)

Is this show in color, or is there something wrong with the set?

SHREVIE (*offscreen*)

This is a black and white set, but I don't think that show is in color, anyway.

43. Interior. Appliance store.

*Another angle—*SHREVIE *and the* CUSTOMER *are standing in an aisle filled with rows o*
televisions.

CUSTOMER

I don't like color television. Don't like that color for nothin'. Saw "Bonanza" at my in-laws; it's not for me. The Ponderosa looked fake. Hardly recognized Little Joe.

SHREVIE

It might have needed some tuning.

CUSTOMER

It's not for me. You got an Emerson? Hear they're real good.

SHREVIE *and the* CUSTOMER *move down the aisle, passing one black and white set after another. One set is in color—"Tom and Jerry" is on the set.* FENWICK *enters the store. He looks slightly drunk.*

SHREVIE

Here's an Emerson. This is portable.

The CUSTOMER *stares at it.* SHREVIE *notices* FENWICK *up at the front of the store. He nods to him.*

CUSTOMER

You got that twenty-one-inch Emerson? The cabinet type?

SHREVIE

The console model.

(*yelling toward the back*)

Kenny! We get some of the Emerson consoles in?!

KENNY (*offscreen*)

Let me check out in the warehouse!

SHREVIE

Be right back. That'll take a minute or two for him to check.

The CUSTOMER *nods, and* SHREVIE *walks up to* FENWICK.

FENWICK

I talked to Boog. He's going to take Carol to the Strand tonight.

SHREVIE

So what do you want to do?

FENWICK

I figure I'll be there. Sit a few seats away.

SHREVIE

Think I'll be there, too. Don't want any judgment calls.

FENWICK

Boog's got about a hundred dollars riding on this thing now. Making bets left and right.

SHREVIE

Jesus, hundred bucks, already?

FENWICK

Lot of people bettin' for Carol.

SHREVIE *senses that* FENWICK *is a little off.*

SHREVIE

What the hell you been doing? You been drinking already?

FENWICK

Yeah? I guess so.

SHREVIE

What for? It's too early.

FENWICK

I don't know. . . . I don't know. Gettin' antsy or something.
Can't figure out what. . . . I don't know.

He turns and starts to head out of the store.

FENWICK (*continuing*)

See you at the Strand.

SHREVIE

Fen, sure you're OK?

FENWICK *turns back and smiles at* SHREVIE.

FENWICK

Hey . . . yeah.

He turns back and exits.

44. Exterior. Street. Day.

EDDIE *parks his Studebaker, and he and* BILLY *exit the car. They walk along a street of
row houses and then cross an old brick street, heading for the pool hall on the corner.*

EDDIE

Colt championship is tomorrow. Want me to get you a ticket
for the game?

BILLY

Can you get one this late?

EDDIE

Yeah. You can't be in Baltimore and not see the Colts win the
championship. It would be sacrilegious.

They enter the pool hall.

Cut to

45. Interior. Pool hall. Day.

BILLY *and* EDDIE *come down the steps into the poolroom. The place is old and dirty looking. Candy wrappers and cigarettes litter the floor.* KNOCKO, *a gray-haired man in his sixties, sits behind the cash register reading* The Wall Street Journal. *On the back wall are pictures of the seminude girls from the men's magazines of the period. Some are inscribed to* KNOCKO. *A TV set is on in the background. A commercial for Renault is seen.*

As the GUYS *approach,* KNOCKO *looks up and smiles.*

> KNOCKO

Billy, Billy, Billy.

> BILLY

How you doing, Knocko?

> KNOCKO

Eat, sleep, you know. Never see you and the guys anymore.

> BILLY

You know how it is. Time to move on, I guess.

> KNOCKO

Eddie's the only one who still pops in. Still loves the game.

> (*very seriously*)

You doing OK, Billy?

> BILLY

Going for my masters.

> KNOCKO

Wonderful. All your crowd turned out fine. Take seven. It's got a new felt.

> EDDIE

Eight's better.

> KNOCKO

Take eight. The pool maven here.

They walk toward the tables. The place is quiet. Afternoons are not the action time.

Cut to

46. Interior. Pool hall. Slightly later.

Tight shot—a pool ball

After a beat EDDIE's *head comes into the frame behind the ball. He closes one eye as he lines up a shot.*

EDDIE

I'm scared shitless, to tell you the truth.

BILLY (*offscreen*)

You know anybody who's not?

EDDIE

If I had a choice, I'd just date Elyse all my life. Just date her and the hell with the rest. I like dating.

47. Interior. Pool hall.

Another angle as EDDIE *backs off the shot and starts to move around the table.* BILLY *sips an orange soda.*

BILLY

What are you doing it for?

EDDIE *approaches* BILLY, *reaches for the bottle, and takes a sip.*

EDDIE

What am I doing it for? I've been dating Elyse for five years. What am I . . . I have no choice. It gets to a point where a girl says, "Hey, where am I going?"

He hands the bottle back and chalks his pool cue.

EDDIE (*continuing*)

So, there is nobody else that I really care about. So, you know. I'm not saying that I'm doing it just to make her happy. The hell with that.

He shoots and sinks a ball.

EDDIE (*continuing*)

She's the only one I care about. I don't go looking for girls to date or anything like that. And, it seems like the time and all . . . so. At least she's not a ball breaker. Christ, if she were a ball breaker, there'd be no way.

BILLY *feels a certain sadness for* EDDIE, *but he doesn't know what to say.*

EDDIE *sees* METHAN, *a blond-haired kid several years younger than he.*

EDDIE (*continuing*)

How you doing, Methan?

METHAN *approaches* EDDIE *and stands inches away from* EDDIE's *face.*

METHAN

"JJ, it's one thing to wear your dog collar, . . . but when it turns
into a noose, . . . I'd rather have my freedom."

BILLY *has no idea what is going on.*

METHAN (*continuing*)

"The man in jail is always for freedom. Except, if you'll excuse
me, JJ, I'm not in jail. You're blind, Mr. McGoo! This is the
crossroads for me. I won't get Kello! Not for a lifetime pass to
the Polo Grounds! Not if you serve me Cleopatra on a plate!
Sidney, I told you . . ."

Suddenly METHAN *walks away, still mumbling the movie.*

METHAN

"And that is why you put your hands on my sister? JJ, please.
. . . Susie tried to throw herself off the terrace. . . . Susie, tell
'im the truth. . . . Tell 'im . . . JJ, please. . . . Look. . . . I can explain.
. . . JJ, . . . stop! Stop! . . . Stop! You're defending your sister,
ya big phony! Didn't you tell me to get Kello? Didn't you
. . . Susie, just as I know he's lying about your attempted suicide,
. . . you know he's lying about me. But we can't leave it like this,
can we? I suggest you go to bed, dear."

EDDIE (*to* BILLY)

Methan's favorite movie. *Sweet Smell of Success.*

BILLY

He memorized the whole movie?

EDDIE *lines up another shot.*

EDDIE

The younger guys, I tell ya, are crazier than we were.

He shoots and misses. From another table a GUY *yells out.*

GUY

Eddie, you taking any of Boogie's action?

EDDIE

Yeah! No way he pulls this off.

48. Exterior. The Strand Theater. Night.

There is a lot of milling around in front of the theater. The marquee reads TROY DONAHUE
AND SANDRA DEE IN SUMMER PLACE.

49. Interior. The Strand Theater lobby. Night.

SHREVIE *stands with* BETH, *an attractive girl.* EDDIE *and* FENWICK *enter and walk over to* SHREVIE.

> SHREVIE (*almost apologizing for bringing* BETH)
> Beth heard the movie was pretty good.

> BETH
> Eddie, where's Elyse?

> EDDIE
> She's home studying for the football test.

> BETH
> You're kidding.

> FENWICK
> Seen the Boog yet?

> SHREVIE
> Not yet.

EARL MAGET, *an enormously fat guy, enters with a* FRIEND. *The* FRIEND *stops at the candy counter.*

> FRIEND
> Earl, want some candy?

> EARL (*starting into the theater*)
> No, don't care for sweets.

BOOGIE *enters with* CAROL HEATHROW. *She is a beautiful, shapely blonde.* BOOGIE *looks over at the group, nods, and walks to the candy counter with* CAROL.

> BETH
> Is that Carol Heathrow?

> SHREVIE
> Where?

> BETH
> With Boogie.

> SHREVIE (*staring for a long beat*)
> I think so.

> BETH
> I'm surprised she's with him. From what I've heard about her,
> Boogie wouldn't seem her type.

EDDIE *is amazed at how beautiful* CAROL *looks.*

EDDIE

She is death. Death.

FENWICK *spots the* GRIPPER *walking toward the men's room. The* GRIPPER *stands about six feet four inches and is all muscle.*

FENWICK

Damn! The Gripper's here.

SHREVIE

Where?

FENWICK *nods toward the men's room.*

SHREVIE (*continuing*)

Christ, the Grip's still growing, I think.

FENWICK

Hope he doesn't see me. Every time he sees me, he puts the grip on me.

EDDIE

Saw him put a grip on a guy at the diner. Gripped him right through his corduroy jacket. Made him stand on tiptoes.

SHREVIE

Where's Billy?

EDDIE

Comin' with that Barbara Kohler chick, I think.

BOOGIE *gets a large box of popcorn and a Coke and starts into the theater with* CAROL. *Just before he enters, he gives a smile to the guys.*

FENWICK

Guess I might as well get a seat.

(*to* EDDIE)

Comin'?

EDDIE *nods, and they start inside. After a beat* SHREVIE *and* BETH *start in.*

SHREVIE

Let's sit in the back.

BETH

Why?

SHREVIE

I'm tired of sittin' down close with the guys and all.

Just as they go into the theater, BILLY *enters alone.*

50. Interior. The Strand Theater.

BOOGIE *and* CAROL *sit watching the screen. The box of popcorn resting in his lap.* BOOGIE *keeps sneaking looks at* CAROL; *then slowly moves his hand down to his fly, and he quietly unzips it.*

51. Interior. The Strand Theater.

Angle to include FENWICK *looking over from his vantage point three seats away.* BOOGIE *squirms around ever so slightly and then places the box of popcorn back on his lap. Evidently he has stuck his penis into the bottom of the popcorn box.* FENWICK *nudges* EDDIE *and then whispers something into his ear.* EDDIE *smiles.*

CAROL *dips her hand into the popcorn box on* BOOGIE's *lap and takes out a handful of popcorn.*

SHREVIE, *seated in the back, is restless, wondering what is happening.* BETH *is mesmerized by Troy Donahue.*

BILLY *sits on an aisle, unaware of the quiet intrigue that is taking place.*

CAROL *again reaches into the box and takes out a few kernels.* BOOGIE *glances toward* FENWICK. FENWICK *shakes his head and mouths, "Bet's off. Not fair."* BOOGIE *nods "yes."*

Troy and Sandra walk the beach. The romantic score swells. The young audience is caught up in this screen love affair.

CAROL *reaches into the popcorn box once again. Suddenly she screams. She bolts up from her seat and races up the aisle. The* AUDIENCE *is alive with chatter, wondering what has happened.*

BOOGIE *turns to* FENWICK *and smiles. Then he heads up the aisle after* CAROL.

      BETH (*as she watches* BOOGIE *racing up the aisle after* CAROL)

BETH

What's going on?

SHREVIE (playing dumb)

I don't know. I don't know.

52. Interior. The Strand Theater lobby.

BOOGIE *catches up to* CAROL *just as she is about to enter the ladies' room.*

BOOGIE

Hold on. Hold on a second.

CAROL

You are disgusting!

                                    BOOGIE

I know it was terrible, really horrible and all, but it was an
accident.

                                    CAROL

An accident!

She starts into the ladies' room. BOOGIE *holds her arm.*

                                    BOOGIE

Wait! Carol! Woo! Seriously, it was an accident. Swear to God.

                                    CAROL

An accident. Your *thing* just got into a box of popcorn?

                                    BOOGIE

Damn near that. Can I be straight with you?

CAROL *tries to settle down.*

                                    CAROL

Boogie . . .

                                    BOOGIE

There's a good reason, but it's a little embarrassing to me. So
maybe you don't want to hear it. I'll understand.

                         CAROL (*a long beat*)

Go on. Let me hear this.

                                    BOOGIE

I don't like to tell this to girls, but you really are a knockout,
really. And, uh, just sitting next to you in there got me crazy.
I got a hard-on. I don't like to admit it, but I did. You don't
know me, but I always try to come off being cool. Don't like
to look like I'm hustling, and there I am, sitting next to you with
a boner. Am I embarrassing you?

                         CAROL (*intrigued*)

Go on.

The "Summer Place *Theme" can be heard softly through the theater doors.*

                                    BOOGIE

Well, it was killing me. So to stop the pain—it was digging into
my pants and all—I opened my fly. Loosen everything up. Give
it a little air, you know. And it worked. Everything settled
down and I got caught up in the picture. Forgot all about it.
Then when I saw Sandra wearing the bathing suit in that cove
scene, you know, it just popped right out and went right

through the bottom of the popcorn box. The force of it opened
the flap.

CAROL *stares at him, wondering whether he is telling the truth. The beautiful theme from*
A Summer Place *grows louder for a few seconds as someone comes through the doors
and heads for the candy counter.*

> CAROL
> It just pushed the flap open?

> BOOGIE
> It's Ripley's, I tell ya. And I couldn't move the box, or you
> would have seen it.

> CAROL
> That's true.

> BOOGIE
> I was just hoping it would shrink back out.

He puts his hand up to her cheek and lovingly touches it.

> BOOGIE
> Come on, let's go back inside.

As they go through the doors, we hear the soundtrack.

> TROY (*voice-over*)
> I want to kiss you here in front of God and everyone.

Cut to

53. Exterior. The Strand Theater. Night.

SHREVIE *and* BETH *exit the theater.*

> SHREVIE
> What was the guy's name? The actor?

> BETH
> Troy Donahue.

> SHREVIE
> What kind of a name is Troy?

> BETH
> He's gorgeous.

> SHREVIE (*mumbling to himself*)
> Troy.

FENWICK *and* EDDIE *approach.*

                        SHREVIE (*continuing*)

Ever hear of a guy named Troy?

                        FENWICK (*sarcastically*)

Yeah, Troy Swartzman from Towanda.

                        SHREVIE

Cute.

BETH *is looking at the poster on the side of the theater.*

                        BETH

Hey, Shrevie, did you know that this movie was written by the author of *The Man in the Gray Flannel Suit*?

                        SHREVIE

No.

                        BETH

You know, I'd really like to see this again.

                        SHREVIE

Well, you can take Elyse.

BOOGIE *and* CAROL *exit the theater.*

                        BOOGIE (*as he passes the* GROUP)

See you guys at the diner. Bring some tens.

BOOGIE *walks on cockily with his arm around* CAROL'*s waist.*

                        BETH

Ten whats?

                        SHREVIE

Have no idea.

EDDIE *looks at* CAROL *as she walks away.*

                        EDDIE

Death.

                        (*to* FENWICK)

I'd give up *your* life if I could have her.

BILLY *exits the theater and starts toward the* CROWD. *Out of the corner of his eye he spots someone exiting through another door. He watches the* GUY *for a beat and then quickly moves toward him. He taps the* GUY *on the shoulder. As the* GUY *turns,* BILLY *punches him in the face. The* GUY *goes down.*

A CROWD *quickly forms. Confusion takes over as everyone moves to see what has happened.* SHREVIE, FENWICK, *and* EDDIE *move in for a better look.*

The GUY *sits on the ground holding his bleeding nose. He looks up at* BILLY.

BILLY

We're even.

BILLY *turns and moves away.* EDDIE, FENWICK, *and* SHREVIE *move to catch up with him.*
BETH *trails along.*

EDDIE

I'll be damned. Willard Broxton!

FENWICK

Long time comin', huh, Billy?

BILLY (*excited*)

I couldn't believe it! There he was! I didn't want to hit him, but
I had to, you know.

SHREVIE (*patting* BILLY's *back*)

Outstanding! See you guys later. Come on, Beth.

BETH

Are we going to eat?

SHREVIE

Nah, not in the mood.

SHREVIE *heads toward his Hudson.* BETH *follows.*

BETH

Who's Willard Broxton?

SHREVIE

It was the eleventh . . . no, tenth grade. Billy was playing ball
against one of the high-school fraternities. I think they were
ULP. Billy came sliding into second base to break up a double
play. The second baseman jumps Billy, thinking he was out to
hurt him. Billy punches the guy and the whole ULP team
jumped him. Beat the shit out of him.

They approach the Hudson. SHREVIE *goes around to the driver's side and opens the door.*

BETH

He's been after them all these years? That was forever ago.

SHREVIE

He swore he'd get them. Broxton makes eight . . . or seven. No,
eight. There's one guy left.

BETH *stands by the car as* SHREVIE *gets in.*

SHREVIE

What are you waiting for? It's open.

Cut to

54. Exterior. Back alley. Night.

BILLY, EDDIE, *and* FENWICK *walk away from the theater toward their cars.*

> FENWICK
>
> I'm so pissed I missed the punch. I was watching out for the Gripper.

> BILLY
>
> Seven years. Seven years to get him.

> EDDIE
>
> Who's the last? Donald Tucker?

> BILLY
>
> No, I got Tucker in a bathroom at Chestnut Ridge. Moon Shaw.

> EDDIE
>
> Moon Shaw.
>
> > (*a beat*)
>
> Who's Moon Shaw?

BILLY *gets in his car.*

> BILLY
>
> If you ever see him, you'll remember.

> EDDIE
>
> Going to the diner?

> BILLY
>
> In a while. I'm going to see Barbara.

> EDDIE
>
> Thought you were supposed to have a date.

> BILLY
>
> She had to work. I'm going to stop by the TV station and see her for a bit.

He starts his car and pulls away.

> FENWICK
>
> Wasn't Moon Shaw the toast who used to date Elaine?

> EDDIE
>
> That was my cousin Denny. You calling him an asshole?

> FENWICK (*knowing he said the wrong thing*)
>
> Oh, . . . not Elaine. Her name was Ellen. I'm thinking a whole other guy.

FENWICK *tiptoes away from* EDDIE, *playing as if he doesn't want to get hit.*

Cut to

55. Interior. Television-station corridor. Night.

BILLY *and* BARBARA *walk down the hallway quickly.* BARBARA *is a tall, thin brunet with classic features. She was never a girl. Born a woman. She moves down the hallway with great purpose.* BILLY *keeps pace.*

> BARBARA
>
> There's not much time before the news.

> BILLY
>
> I tried to call.

> BARBARA
>
> Switchboard closes down at ten.

> BILLY
>
> I was just getting the feeling you were avoiding me, Barb.

> BARBARA
>
> That's not true, Willy.

They enter the control room.

56. Interior. Television-station control room.

The control room overlooks the studio floor. Technicians are setting up the cameras, microphones, and lights. A bank of monitors hangs down from a metal shelf. The TECHNICAL DIRECTOR *is talking over a headset, balancing video levels.* BARBARA *slips on a headset and shuffles through some papers.*

> BARBARA (*into the headset*)
>
> Telecine, you want to run down the film chains for me?

BILLY *takes in all the activity. He is overwhelmed. His eye catches the Old Gold dancing boxes on one of the monitors.*

> BARBARA (*continuing; getting information*)
>
> Governor's press conference is on three? There's a B-roll to that.
> Four? OK. Goodwill charity Christmas party? Three also? And
> the slides? One?

BARBARA *looks up at the clock. It reads 10:58. The* DIRECTOR *rushes into the booth with the news script. He quickly sits and puts on his headset.*

> DIRECTOR
>
> Stand by for cold tease.

BARBARA

Ten seconds.

BILLY *steps forward to get a better view of the activity on the floor. The* DIRECTOR *becomes aware of his presence.*

DIRECTOR

Who's the visitor?

BARBARA

Friend of mine. Five seconds.

DIRECTOR

And one. Mike. Cue!

NEWSCASTER

President Eisenhower returns from world peace tour. Steel dispute continues. These and other stories next.

DIRECTOR

Roll three. Three and track.

A commercial comes up on the air monitor.

BARBARA

Willy, after this I still have a lot of work to do. Why don't you call in the morning?

DIRECTOR

Where's the news opening?

BARBARA

On six.

BILLY

What's good?

BARBARA

Church services are at ten; eight thirty, nine.

DIRECTOR

Punch ID and announce.

A slide of the television-station's call letters comes up. The ANNOUNCER *in a glass booth off to the right speaks.*

ANNOUNCER

This is WMAR-TV 2 in Baltimore, wishing all our viewers a merry Christmas and a happy New Year.

Cut to

57. Exterior. Saint Agnes's Church. Night.

A nativity scene is set up on the grounds. Wonderfully elaborate, it is about half life-size. The figures are made of clay and painted in fine detail. The camera pans over to FENWICK, *who is parked nearby. He leans on his Triumph, holding a half-pint of whiskey. He takes a big swig and shivers slightly. The air is cold, and his breath comes out in white puffs.*

Cut to

58. Exterior. Diner. Night.

EDDIE *and* SHREVIE *lean against a car parked in front of the hangout. The diner's blue neon sign above reflects off the cars, bathing the* GUYS *in a cold, blue light.*

> EDDIE
>
> Two days till the test. If she passes, three more days to the thing
> . . . the marriage.

> SHREVIE
>
> Where you going? Puerto Rico?

> EDDIE
>
> Cuba.

> SHREVIE
>
> My parents' friends, the Copelands, go every year. Nice.

There is a long pause.

> EDDIE
>
> Shrevie, you happy with your marriage, or what?

> SHREVIE
>
> To be honest, I don't know.

> EDDIE
>
> You know. How can you *not* know? It's not like you're trying
> to figure out the difference between Pepsi Cola and Royal
> Crown, for Christsake.

> SHREVIE
>
> Beth is terrific and everything, but I don't know.

EDDIE *looks off, not happy with the answer.*

> SHREVIE (*continuing*)
>
> You know the big part of the problem? When we were dating,
> we spent most of our time talking about sex. *Why* couldn't I do
> it? *Where* could we do it? Were her parents going to be out *so*

we could do it. Talking about being alone for a weekend. A whole night. You know. Everything was talking about gettin' sex or planning our wedding. Then when you're married, . . . it's crazy. You can have it whenever you want. You wake up. She's there. You come home from work. She's there. So, all the sex-planning talk is over. And the wedding-planning talk. We can sit up here and bullshit the night away, but I can't have a five-minute conversation with Beth. But, I'm not putting the blame on her. We've just got nothing to talk about.

EDDIE *lights a Pall Mall.*

> EDDIE
>
> Well, that's OK. We've got the diner.

> SHREVIE
>
> Yeah, we've always got the diner. Don't worry about it.

> EDDIE
>
> I'm not worried.

> SHREVIE
>
> Don't back out on me.

> EDDIE
>
> I'm not going to back out on you either, unless she fails the test. It's out of my hands.

Cut to

59. Exterior. Heathrows' house. Night.

The house is a pleasant, two-story wooden structure. A yellow porch light is on. BOOGIE *and* CAROL *walk up the steps to the front door.* CAROL *opens the door with the key. She turns back toward* BOOGIE.

> BOOGIE (*softly*)
>
> I love you.

He gently kisses her forehead, then looks her in the eyes. CAROL *throws her arms around his neck and kisses him passionately.*

> CAROL
>
> Do you want to come inside?

> BOOGIE
>
> Are your parents around?

CAROL

They're probably in the basement watching TV.

BOOGIE

I'd love to, but I really should hit the law books. OK?

CAROL *nods. He strokes her cheek.*

BOOGIE (*continuing*)

I wish I could stay.

CAROL

Talk to you. Soon?

BOOGIE *nods and walks away.* CAROL *watches him with great affection; then she turns and enters the house.*

Cut to

60. Exterior. Diner. Night.

FENWICK *pulls over to the curb across the street from the diner. He exits the car.* EDDIE, SHREVIE, MODELL, *and a* GROUP *of others are all hanging out. A voice calls out—a soft, but very authoritative voice.*

VOICE

Whaddya say, Tim?

FENWICK *turns.* THE GRIPPER *is standing by his car.*

FENWICK

Whaddya say, Gripper?

GRIPPER

Not much, Tim.

He moves toward him ever so slowly.

FENWICK

Oh no, you're not going to put the grip on me.

GRIPPER

Where do you get that idea, Tim?

FENWICK *backs up; then he suddenly rips the antenna off his car and waves it like a sword.*

FENWICK

No! Stay away! I'm not going to get gripped! You're not going to get me to walk on my tiptoes in pain. Oh, no.

GRIPPER (*even more softly*)

Tim, I'm not going to grip you.

FENWICK (*waving the antenna*)

Yes, you are.

The GUYS *across the street are loving what is happening.*

GRIPPER

To be honest, I was. But not now. I like a guy who stands up to the Gripper. I like that, Tim.

FENWICK

You're not going to grip me?

GRIPPER

No, I just want to shake your hand.

FENWICK

You're settin' me up for a grip.

GRIPPER

Untrue, Tim.

FENWICK

Sure?

GRIPPER

I want to shake the hand of the man who stood up to the Gripper.

FENWICK

No grip?

GRIPPER

That's right, Tim.

FENWICK *drops the antenna. He moves toward* THE GRIPPER *slowly.* THE GRIPPER *extends his hand;* FENWICK *extends his hand. They shake. No grip.* FENWICK *is relieved.*

GRIPPER (*continuing*)

Let's go see the guys. The man who stood up to the Gripper.

FENWICK, *feeling very proud, walks with* THE GRIPPER *across the street toward the* GUYS. *Suddenly, halfway across the street,* THE GRIPPER *puts one of the greatest grips in his career on* FENWICK. *He squeezes* FENWICK's *forearm right through his winter coat.* FENWICK *feels the pain. The famous grip is on.*

GRIPPER (*continuing*)

Up on your toes, Tim.

FENWICK

Oh no, Grip.

GRIPPER *puts on a little more pressure, and* FENWICK *is up on his toes. The* GUYS *cheer* GRIPPER.

GRIPPER

Tim, never doubt the Gripper. When I say I want to shake your hand, believe what I say. Never doubt, Tim.

FENWICK

Never doubt. Right.

THE GRIPPER *turns* FENWICK *around and leads him away from the* GUYS, *back to the other side of the street.* FENWICK *is up on his toes. The* GUYS *are eating it up. Then* THE GRIPPER *and* FENWICK *head back to the* GUYS. *The camera pans to* BOOGIE'S *car as it pulls into the parking lot on the left side of the building. He starts to pass* BAGEL, *who is about to drive out.* BAGEL *beeps his horn and rolls down the window.* BOOGIE *rolls his down.*

BAGEL

Did you hear? They won by fourteen.

BOOGIE

Fourteen? Shit. They weren't supposed to roll up that big a score.

BAGEL

Listen to me next time.

He pulls out. BOOGIE *pulls forward and parks. He slams his fist into the steering wheel. Again and again. Then he leans back in his car seat. He takes a deep breath and gets out of the car.*

61. Exterior. Diner.

Angle on car outside diner with GUYS *hanging around it*
TABACK *has the trunk of his car open and is trying to sell clothes. He grabs one of the* YOUNG GUYS.

TABACK

Hey you! Big time. Come here. Your mother let you loose like this? Look at them pants. I got charcoal pants here.

The KID *draws back.*

TABACK (*continuing*)

You want to get inside the diner? Come here. Look at these charcoal-gray pants. Special sale twelve fifty.

KID

Twelve fifty?

TABACK

All right. For you, eleven ninety-eight. Look, don't tell anybody where you got these, OK? How much money you got.

KID

Four bucks.

TABACK (*delving into his trunk*)

Come here, I got a good shirt for you.

62. Interior. Diner. Later.

EARL MAGET *sits in a booth alone, his enormous body taking up about one whole side. He finishes off one section of a club sandwich and very politely wipes his mouth with a napkin. Before him five deluxe sandwiches are waiting for his hungry mouth. He turns the financial page and picks up another sandwich.*

EDDIE, BILLY, *and* MODELL *are turned around in their booth watching* MAGET. BOOGIE, FENWICK, *and* SHREVIE *are discussing the pecker-in-the-popcorn bet.*

EDDIE (*watching* EARL)

Where's he now?

MODELL (*looking over the menu*)

He's on the Pimlico.

(*surveying the table*)

That's the George's Deluxe. The Garrison, The Avalon, and The Junction.

EDDIE (*amazed*)

The whole left side of the menu. What a triumph if he pulls it off.

MODELL *starts counting the sandwiches on the left side of the menu. We catch snatches of* BOOGIE, FENWICK, *and* SHREVIE *arguing.*

FENWICK

The bet was touch your pecker. Not pecker hidden in popcorn.

SHREVIE

It was pecker touching without intention.

BOOGIE

Listen to this.

MODELL *looks up from the menu.*

MODELL

Fifteen . . . or sixteen more. If you include the Maryland fried-chicken dinner.

EDDIE

I think he's just talking deluxe sandwiches.

MODELL (*yelling over*)

Earl! That include the fried-chicken dinner?

EARL

Yes.

EDDIE (*truly amazed*)

Twenty-two deluxe sandwiches *and* the fried-chicken dinner.

BILLY

And no bets.

EDDIE

Nope. Just a personal goal. Another private triumph. This'll top the eighty White Tower hamburgers.

MODELL

Unbelievable . . . like a building with feet.

BILLY

He ate eighty White Tower hamburgers?

EDDIE

Oh yeah, you didn't know? Thanksgiving night. Eighty-six he ate. Saw him later and said, 'Earl, your goal was eighty. Why eighty-six?' He looked at me and said, 'I got hungry.'

BILLY *laughs.*

MODELL

Truth.

They slide back down in the booth.

SHREVIE (*to* BOOGIE)

But it was a trick. I don't buy it.

EDDIE (*joining in the conversation*)

Me either. I want it on the up and up. Default.

BOOGIE

Let it all ride. Tell you what.

BOOGIE *stirs his french fry in the gravy for a long beat. The guys eagerly await his proposal.*

                              BOOGIE (*continuing*)
I bet I ball Carol Heathrow on the next date.

                              FENWICK
Now you're nuts.

                              BOOGIE
Fifty bucks a guy.

                              EDDIE
Fifty?

                              SHREVIE
It's like stealing money from you, Boog.

                              BOOGIE
In?

The guys all take the bet except BILLY.

                              BOOGIE (*continuing*)
And I'll take all the action I can get.

                              FENWICK
We need validation.

                              BOOGIE
I'll arrange it. You want to be there to validate?

                              FENWICK
Sure.

There's a slight sense of anxiety in BOOGIE's *attitude.* BILLY *picks up on it.*
Cut to

63. Exterior. Diner. Night.

The first rays of morning light reflect off the diner's front windows. EARL MAGET *exits. The*
GUYS *follow behind, applauding as he goes.*

MAGET *calmly crosses the parking lot, gets into his little, yellow Nash Metropolitan, and*
drives off.

                              SHREVIE
You all want to meet here and go to the game in my car?

                              BOOGIE
Yeah, that's good.

                              SHREVIE (*getting into his car*)
Meet here at twelve.

EDDIE

Make it quarter to. Don't want to miss any of the pregame shit.

SHREVIE

Why don't you go now? Then you'll be sure not to miss anything.

He starts his car.

EDDIE

We're talking the championship game. Quarter to.

SHREVIE *nods. The* GUYS *all exchange see ya's, get into their cars, and drive off. The diner parking lot is now empty except for* FENWICK's *Triumph.*

Cut to

64. Exterior. Countryside. Day.

The morning sun is up now. A very attractive GIRL *in full riding gear gallops along on a chestnut stallion. She rides expertly, seemingly unaffected by the cold morning air.*

The camera pulls back until we see BOOGIE's *cherry and white DeSoto keeping pace on the road close by.*

65. Interior. Boogie's car. Day.

BOOGIE

I've got to meet this girl. She is *death!*

FENWICK

Very nice.

BOOGIE

I'm in love.

66. Exterior. Countryside. Day.

BOOGIE's *car continues to trail alongside the* GIRL *on the horse.* BOOGIE *rolls down the window.*

BOOGIE (*yelling out*)

Miss! Miss! Woo! Miss!

The GIRL *pulls up on the reins and stops.* BOOGIE *quickly steps out of the car and approaches.*

GIRL

Yes.

BOOGIE *is amazed. She's more beautiful up close—long, black hair and deep, blue eyes— elegant.*

> BOOGIE
>
> I was admiring your horse.

> GIRL *(very reserved)*
>
> Were you?

> BOOGIE
>
> Do you ride western style as well?

FENWICK *gets out of the car and leans against the door.*

> GIRL
>
> I do, but I prefer English. There's a finer sense of control.

> BOOGIE
>
> What's your name?

> GIRL
>
> Jane Chisolm.

> GIRL *(continuing, as* BOOGIE *stares)*
>
> As in the Chisholm Trail.

She gallops away. BOOGIE *watches her go for a beat and then turns to* FENWICK.

> BOOGIE
>
> What fuckin' Chisholm Trail?

He walks back to the car and gets inside. FENWICK *does the same.*

67. Interior. Boogie's car. Day.

> FENWICK
>
> You get the feeling there's something going on that we don't know about?

> BOOGIE
>
> You get the feeling she gave me a false name?
>
> *(starting up the car)*
>
> Want to drive some more?

> FENWICK
>
> Naw, let's call it a night.

68. Exterior. Countryside. Day.

BOOGIE's *DeSoto drives off, white picket fences framing the car as it heads down the road. We hear the sound of church bells.*

Cut to

69. Exterior. Saint Agnes's Church. Day.

The bells in the tower ring. BILLY *sits in his car waiting for* BARBARA. *Members of the congregation walk down the path, passing the nativity scene off to the left.*

BILLY *watches for* BARBARA. *The crowd thins. He exits his car and walks toward the church looking around, thinking he may have missed her somehow. He peeks inside the church, unsure whether to enter. A* CHURCH MEMBER *exits.*

> BILLY
>
> Is there anyone inside?

> CHURCH MEMBER
>
> I didn't notice.

> BILLY
>
> Is it all right to go in?

> CHURCH MEMBER
>
> Of course.

BILLY *enters.*

Cut to

70. Interior. Saint Agnes's Church. Day.

BILLY *stands at the back and looks around the large, stone structure. He sees* BARBARA *still sitting, all alone. He goes down the aisle quietly and joins her in the pew.*

> BILLY
>
> Anything wrong, Barb?

> BARBARA
>
> No.
>
> (*a long pause*)
>
> Yes. I think I'm pregnant.

> BILLY (*a long pause*)
>
> Me?

BARBARA

Yes. Our one day in New York last month. Six years of a platonic relationship, then one night of sex, . . . and this happens.

They sit silently.

BILLY

Maybe it's for the best.

BARBARA

No, . . . I don't think so. Do you want to marry me?

BILLY

Yes.

BARBARA

Is that why you came back a few days early? To ask?

BILLY

I thought after New York, you know. Seven weeks is a long time when you miss someone.

BARBARA

New York was a mistake.

BILLY

Maybe it wasn't as romantic as we'd like it to be, but I think it will happen. It's not perfect, yet, but, . . . I love you, Barb.

BARBARA

You're confusing a friendship with a woman and love. It's not the same.

They sit saying nothing.

Cut to

71. Exterior. Memorial Stadium. Day.

Aerial view moving toward the main tower of the stadium. We hear the CROWD *yell,* "C!!! O!!!" *We move closer to the tower. The* CROWD *roars,* "L!!! T!!!" *We keep moving closer.* "S!!!" *We pass over the tower and enter the stadium. A deafening crowd roar is heard:* "COLTS!!!"

Cut to

72. Interior. Memorial Stadium. Day.

A COLT DEFENSIVE LINEMAN *smashes into the* GIANT'S QUARTERBACK, *knocking him to the ground with a thud. The* COLTS *are fired up. The championship is within their grasp.*

73. Interior. Memorial Stadium.

The scoreboard reads:
GIANTS *16*   COLTS *31.*

74. Interior. Memorial Stadium.

Angle on EDDIE, BILLY, SHREVIE, BOOGIE *and* FENWICK. *They are on their feet. Victory is minutes away.*

                              EDDIE (*yelling*)
Gino! Gino!

                                (*to* BILLY)
He's incredible. They should build a statue, a monument to
him. Something, you know.

SHREVIE *takes the binoculars from* BOOGIE *and looks through them.*

                              SHREVIE
Which one?

                              BOOGIE
Second from the right.

75. Interior. Memorial Stadium.

SHREVIE'*s point of view, through the binoculars. We see a* CHEERLEADER. *Then the camera pans to* ANOTHER CHEERLEADER.

                        BOOGIE (*offscreen*)
See her?

                        SHREVIE (*offscreen*)
Yeah. How can you tell she's not wearing panties?

76. Interior. Memorial Stadium.

Back to the GUYS. SHREVIE *puts down the binoculars.*

                              BOOGIE
You have to wait for her to jump.

SHREVIE

And when she jumped, you saw?

BOOGIE

I see everything.

SHREVIE *puts the glasses to his eyes again.*

SHREVIE

Come on! Jump!

BOOGIE *smiles at* FENWICK. FENWICK *holds back a laugh.*

FENWICK

I think there's a jump coming up.

The COLTS *take possession of the ball and start to run the clock down.*

EDDIE

More points! Johnny, the bomb!

BILLY

Ed, we've got it wrapped up.

EDDIE

I don't want just a win. I want humiliation. Goddamn New
York teams think they're hot shit.

(*yelling out*)

Humiliation! Johnny, humiliation!

The CHEERLEADERS *give a big cheer.*

FENWICK

Quick, Shrevie. She's going to jump.

SHREVIE *quickly starts to bring the binoculars to his eyes, but* BOOGIE *has his arm through
the strap.*

BOOGIE

Oops. Wait a second.

SHREVIE *tries to untangle* BOOGIE's *arm.*

FENWICK

Too late.

SHREVIE *stares at* BOOGIE *a beat and then realizes he's been hustled.*

SHREVIE

Very good. Very good.

The scoreboard clock ticks. The CROWD *counts down the seconds. "FIVE . . . FOUR
. . . THREE . . . TWO . . . ONE." Pandemonium. The* GUYS *go crazy, grabbing and
hugging one another.*

Some of the CROWD *starts to swarm onto the field. The* GUYS *follow.*

The late afternoon sun has dropped below the stands. The lights are on. A gray-golden haze envelops the field.

FANS *are trying to tear down the goalpost.* BILLY, EDDIE, SHREVIE, BOOGIE, *and* FENWICK *hang from the goalpost singing the Baltimore Colt fight song. There may be happier days ahead for the* GUYS, *but this one will be hard to beat. The goalpost finally comes apart, and the* GUYS *fall to the ground in a heap laughing happily.*

Cut to

77. Interior. Fenwick's apartment. Night.

FENWICK *sits watching ''GE College Bowl,'' the quiz show that pits one college team against another. It's a game of intellectual skill.*

The camera pans the apartment. It is imaginatively decorated in pink and turquoise. Five pink flamingos, four feet high, are placed around the room.

TV QUIZ MASTER
That's the opening whistle, and our game begins. Where you're still playing for a thirty-point bonus question, here's another toss-up in English. Are you ready? A spaceship is stranded on the planet Mercury outside of the libration areas; it's night and pitch black outside. For ten points, how long must the explorers wait until sunrise?

FENWICK
The sun doesn't rise on Mercury.

A buzzer sounds.

TV QUIZ MASTER
Bryn Mawr, Stebbins.

STEBBINS
They won't get a sunrise, because Mercury has one side perpetually turned toward the sun and the other side away from the sun.

FENWICK *licks his finger and draws a 1 in the air.*

FENWICK
Hey, Fenwick. Hey, hey.

TV QUIZ MASTER
That's right. They would have to wait forever. That's the answer.

(beat)

I have a twenty-point bonus coming up. Here's a toss-up. For ten points, what would a man probably have if he had a visual zygomatic contusion arch.

FENWICK

Black eye.

A buzzer sounds.

TV QUIZ MASTER

Cornell.

CORNELL TEAM LEADER

Sharp bump on his head.

FENWICK

Black eye! Black eye, you bozo.

TV QUIZ MASTER

No.

STEBBINS

He would have a bump here.

She indicates above her eyebrow.

FENWICK

You look like you've got a bump on your head! A black eye!

TV QUIZ MASTER

We were looking for a black eye, but I'll accept a bruised z-bone.

Cut to

78. Interior. Fenwick's bedroom.

The room is black. More pink flamingos are present. BOOGIE *is talking on the phone. Through the wall we hear the "GE College Bowl" and* FENWICK's *answers.*

BOOGIE

Yeah, Ma, I know I owe two thousand dollars. Guess what? I heard it before you. What am I going to do? I'm choice. Got to find a way to pay it off. Me? I've got fifty-six dollars to my name. Yes, I know I'm in trouble. Then they'll kill me. What can I tell you?

Cut back to

79. Interior. Fenwick's living room.

TV QUIZ MASTER

Here's your toss-up for twenty points. What homegrown phi-
losopher said, "The mass of men lead lives . . . "?

FENWICK

Thoreau.

A buzzer sounds.

TV QUIZ MASTER

Cornell, Pearlman.

PEARLMAN

Thoreau.

QUIZ MASTER

Right, Cornell.

FENWICK *looks smug.*

Cut back to

80. Interior. Fenwick's bedroom.

BOOGIE *sits looking worried. We hear the TV in the background.*

Cut back to

81. Interior. Fenwick's living room.

The quiz show continues.

TV QUIZ MASTER

That's right for ten points. Now you all know the insignia
inscribed on the U.S. Post Office: "Neither snow nor rain nor
heat nor gloom of night . . ."

FENWICK

Herodotus.

TV QUIZ MASTER

What classical author wrote it?

A buzzer sounds.

FENWICK

Hey, Cornell, . . . take a walk, bozo.

BOOGIE *comes into the living room.*

BOOGIE
Talked to Shrevie. He's going to lend me two hundred.

FENWICK
Going over now?

BOOGIE
Yeah.

FENWICK
I'm going to drop in on my brother. Might be able to get some bucks from the toast.

BOOGIE
Howard? Really?

FENWICK *shrugs his shoulders.*

BOOGIE *(continuing, with real sincerity)*
I appreciate that, Fen. I know how you guys feel about one another.

FENWICK *waves him off. He doesn't like any form of praise.* BOOGIE *starts for the door.*

BOOGIE *(continuing)*
With the Heathrow bet and all, I should be close. See ya.

He exits.

Cut to

82. Interior. Shrevie and Beth's house. Night.

A 45-rpm record drops down the spindle. The arm comes forward and gently rests on the record. A rock-and-roll song starts to play.

SHREVIE *is looking through his extremely large record rack. Something is bothering him. He pulls out one record, then another.*

SHREVIE
Beth! Beth!

BETH *is in another room.*

BETH *(offscreen)*
What?

SHREVIE
Come here!

BETH *(offscreen)*
I'm working on a crossword puzzle.

SHREVIE

Come here!

BETH *sticks her head in.*

BETH

What?

SHREVIE

Have you been playing my records?

BETH

Yeah. So?

SHREVIE

Didn't I tell you the procedure?

They have had this discussion before.

BETH

Yes. You told me all about it, Shrevie. They have to be in alphabetical order.

SHREVIE (*like a teacher to a student*)

And what else?

BETH

They have to be filed according to year as well. Alphabetically and according to year. OK?

SHREVIE

And what else?

BETH *thinks.*

SHREVIE (*continuing*)

And what else?

BETH (*confused, then angry*)

I don't know!

SHREVIE

Let me give you a hint. I found James Brown filed under the *J*'s instead of the *B*'s; but to top it off, you put him in the rock-and-roll section! Instead of the R-and-B section! How could you do that?!

BETH

It's too complicated! Every time I pull out a record, there's a whole procedure to go through. I just want to hear music; that's all!

> SHREVIE

Is it too much to keep records in a category? R and B with R and B. Rock and roll with rock and roll. You wouldn't put Charlie Parker with rock and roll, would you?

BETH *says nothing.*

> SHREVIE (*continuing*)

Would you?!!

> BETH

I don't know! Who's Charlie Parker?

> SHREVIE (*exasperated*)

Jazz!! Jazz!! Jazz!!!!

> BETH

What are you getting so crazy about? It's only music. It's not that big a deal.

> SHREVIE

It is! Don't you understand that?! It's important to me!

They stare at one another. SHREVIE *is trying to control his temper.* BETH's *eyes become watery.*

> BETH (*holding back tears*)

Why do you yell at me? I never see you yell at your friends.

> SHREVIE

Pick a record. Any record.

> BETH

What?

> SHREVIE

Pick a record!

BETH *moves to the record rack and pulls out a record. She holds onto it, not sure what* SHREVIE *wants.*

> SHREVIE (*continuing*)

What's the hit side?

> BETH

"Good Golly Miss Molly."

> SHREVIE

Ask me what's on the flip side?

> BETH

Why?

SHREVIE

Ask me what's on the flip side.

BETH

What's on the flip side?

SHREVIE

"Hey, Hey, Hey, Hey"—1958—Specialty Records. You never ask me what's on the flip side!

BETH

Because I don't give a shit! Who cares about the flip side?!

SHREVIE

I do!

He gently thumbs through a handful of records.

SHREVIE *(continuing)*

Every one of these means something. The label. The producer. The year they were made. Who was copying whose style or expanding on it. I hear these, and they bring back certain times in my life.

He stares at her coldly.

SHREVIE *(continuing)*

Don't ever touch these again. Ever.

He starts out of the room. He turns back to BETH.

SHREVIE *(continuing)*

I first met you at Modell's sister's high-school graduation party. 1955. "Ain't That a Shame" was playing as I walked in the door.

He exits and slams the door shut.

Cut to

83. Exterior. Residential street. Night.

BOOGIE *drives down the quiet street and pulls over in front of* SHREVIE's *modest duplex. He quietly gets out of his DeSoto and walks up to the front door. He rings the doorbell and waits.* BETH *opens the door. She holds some Kleenex in her hand.*

BETH

Oh, hi, Boogie.

He notices that she looks upset but says nothing.

                                   BOOGIE

Shrevie here?

                                    BETH

No.

                                   BOOGIE

Is he coming back soon? I talked with him a little while ago.
Said he'd be in.

                                    BETH

I don't know.

She starts to cry. BOOGIE *puts his arms around her and holds her close.*

                                   BOOGIE

What's wrong, babe?

                                    BETH

He ever yell at you?

                                   BOOGIE

What?

                         BETH (*choking back her tears*)

I don't know what to do. We've got a real problem.

                         BOOGIE (*stroking her hair*)

Go on, cry. Just cry, babe.

They stand in the doorway, BETH *crying uncontrollably and* BOOGIE *holding her, comforting her.*

Cut to

84. Interior Shrevie's car. Night.

SHREVIE *drives along in his car, singing with the radio.*

85. Exterior. Fenwick's brother's house. Night.

FENWICK *and his older brother,* HOWARD, *stand in the driveway arguing. It is dark, the main source of light coming from a wrought-iron lamppost on the property. The house is large and very modern in design. Through the picture window we see small* CHILDREN *at play in the living room.*

                                  FENWICK

He's in trouble. Don't you know about friendship, Howard?

HOWARD

Five hundred dollars?

FENWICK

Four hundred, three hundred. Whatever you can afford.

HOWARD

Maybe this is a lesson for you. If you worked, you would have some money to lend him.

FENWICK

Yeah, I know. I'm irresponsible. Dropped out of college. Won't work in the family business. I'm a disgrace. That's a good reason for keeping me out of your house, God knows.

HOWARD

You're a bad example.

FENWICK

Far be it from me to disagree. Give me some money, Howard.

HOWARD

You ever read a book?

FENWICK

Huh?

HOWARD

Read. Do you ever read?

FENWICK

Never.

HOWARD

You should read Dale Carnegie's *How to Win Friends and Influence People*.

FENWICK

I have it on my night table. It's right under *How to Wax Your Car*. Give me some money, Howard.

HOWARD

Where did you get this attitude?

FENWICK

I borrowed it. Have to have it back by midnight. Howard.

FENWICK *starts to pace the driveway. His anger is building.*

HOWARD

I should talk to Daddy about stopping your trust fund. It's killing your initiative.

FENWICK

Big trust fund. One hundred dollars a month until I'm twenty-
three. Granddad was a real Rockefeller.

Suddenly FENWICK *lunges at his* BROTHER, *grabbing his overcoat by the lapels and pushing
him up against the lamppost.*

FENWICK (*continuing*)

Howard, it's important. I wouldn't come otherwise. I don't like
to see you, so you know it's very important.

HOWARD

Get off.

FENWICK

I despise you, and yet I'm here.

HOWARD

Get off.

FENWICK *lets go of him and starts toward his car.*

FENWICK

Funny. As a little kid I always wanted a brother. I told that to
Mom once. She said, "You *have* a brother." I said, "Oh, that's
who the asshole in the other bed is."

FENWICK *gets into his Triumph and pulls away.* HOWARD *shakes his head in disgust.*

Cut to

86. Exterior. A movie theater. Night.

EDDIE *and* BILLY *walk toward the theater. The marquee reads* SEVENTH SEAL.

EDDIE

So what are you going to do?

BILLY

It's up to her.

EDDIE

Her? You've got a big decision to make. We could make it a
double wedding.

They reach the box office, hand over a dollar apiece, and receive two tickets in return.

Cut to

87. Interior. The theater lobby. Night.

EDDIE *notices that there is no candy counter, no popcorn, and the only beverage served is coffee.*

> EDDIE
>
> What the hell's going on here? Nothing to eat.

> BILLY
>
> It's an art theater.

> EDDIE (*throwing* BILLY *a look*)
>
> Fuck art. They oughta get some popcorn in here.

They head into the theater.

Cut to

88. Interior. The theater.

The film is in progress. It's a "heavy" Bergman film, and the scene they're watching is very abstract.

> EDDIE
>
> What am I watching? It just started, and I don't know what's happening.

> BILLY
>
> It's symbolic.

> EDDIE
>
> Yeah?

He gives BILLY *the jerk-off motion. They continue to watch the movie.*

> EDDIE
>
> Who's that guy?

> BILLY
>
> That's Death walking on the beach.

> EDDIE
>
> I've been to Atlantic City a hundred times, and I've never seen Death walk on the beach.

89. Exterior. Saint Agnes's Church. Night.

The nativity scene—the camera pans the faces of the three wise men and then comes to rest on FENWICK's *face. After a beat his half-pint comes into view, and he takes a swig. He shakes his head in disgust.*

As we move back, we see that the baby Jesus is gone. FENWICK *is very bothered by this.*

FENWICK

Kids. Kids did this. A sacrilege for Christsake.

He sits down on the hay next to one of the sheep. He takes another swig on the bottle.

Cut to

90. Interior. Shrevie's car. Night.

SHREVIE *drives along, still coming down from his fight with* BETH. *As he moves along, we see Saint Agnes's on the right up ahead. The nativity display cannot be seen clearly. We move closer and closer.*

SHREVIE *notices something unusual. Out of curiosity he pays closer attention.*

We see the nativity scene more clearly now. Everything is the same except FENWICK *has replaced the baby Jesus. He lies there next to the figure of Mary in his Jockey shorts. Because of the scale of the display,* FENWICK *looks like an enormous baby.*

SHREVIE *slams on his brakes and pulls over to the curb. He quickly gets out of the Hudson and walks up the slope toward the manger.*

Cut to

91. Interior. Movie theater.

EDDIE *is bored to death. He sits in the chair, his eyes drooping, fighting to stay awake.* BILLY *is completely involved. Suddenly a light flashes on them. They turn toward the source.*

An USHER *stands holding a flashlight.* SHREVIE *is with him.*

SHREVIE (to the USHER)

That's the guys.

(to BILLY and EDDIE)

Come on! Emergency!

BILLY

What is it?

SHREVIE

Come on!!

The GUYS *get up quickly.*

EDDIE

What's wrong?

SHREVIE

Fenwick's in the manger.

BILLY (*as they head down the aisle*)

What?

SHREVIE

He's in the manger, and he won't leave.

EDDIE

The manger?

SHREVIE

I've never seen him like this.

They exit through the swinging door to the lobby.

Cut to

92. Exterior. Saint Agnes's Church. Night.

FENWICK *lies happily in the manger, sprawled out in the hay. Although he is almost naked, he seems immune to the cold night air. His bottle certainly helps as a warmer, however. He hums, "Oh, Little Town of Bethlehem."*

The GUYS *come across the church grounds.* FENWICK *sees them and smiles.*

FENWICK

Come, three more wise men. You've heard of the miracle.

EDDIE

Let's go, Fen.

FENWICK

You must have traveled far. Rest your weary feet.

BILLY

The police will be here. Somebody's going to spot you.

FENWICK

This is a big smile, don't you think?

SHREVIE

Yeah, come on.

The GUYS *prod him on.* FENWICK *will have none of it.* BILLY *reaches down to help* FENWICK *up.*

FENWICK (*pushing him away*)

No!

EDDIE *and* SHREVIE *try to help out.* FENWICK *struggles with them. He grabs hold of a wise man.* BILLY *tries to pull him off it. The wise man topples over. The* GUYS *continue to struggle with him.* BILLY *is knocked backward, and part of the structure falls down.*

Cut to

93. Interior. Police car. Night.

Two MEN *drive along, patrolling the street. Off to the right they see what is happening in the nativity display. It looks as if a riot has broken out in the manger. A sheep suddenly sails through the air. The siren wails.*

94. Exterior. Saint Agnes's Church. Night.

The GUYS *are still struggling with* FENWICK. *Everything is a mess. They hear the siren, and the activity quickly comes to a halt.*

As the POLICE *approach, the* GUYS *stand very still. The three* GUYS *are standing side by side.* FENWICK *is in the hay. It looks oddly like a new version of the nativity.*

> EDDIE (*out of the side of his mouth*)
> What do we do?

> BILLY
> Choice.

Cut to

95. Interior. Lockup. Night.

FENWICK *is in a cell alone.* EDDIE *and* SHREVIE *are in the cell next to him.* BILLY *is directly across from them, locked up with another* GUY. *The lights are low.* FENWICK *and* SHREVIE *are asleep.* BILLY *and* EDDIE *stand by the bars talking to one another.*

> EDDIE
> I added a couple killer questions to the test. Tomorrow night's the showdown.

> BILLY
> She studying hard?

> EDDIE
> Better be. Otherwise she's off to Cuba alone.

> BILLY
> Wish I knew what to do about Barbara.

The CELLMATE *starts putting his fingers in* BILLY's *hair.* BILLY *pushes him away. He tries to ignore him.*

EDDIE

Get married. Take her back to school. Get a part-time job. By the time the kid arrives, you'll have your masters, and all's well.

BILLY

And what about her job?

EDDIE

Her job? I give you an answer, and you confuse it by bringing her into the problem.

BILLY *pushes the* GUY *away again.*

BILLY (*to the cellmate*)

Take a walk.

(*to* EDDIE)

Ed, she's in this thing. There's two of us. She loves her work, and . . . and she doesn't want to marry me. That's the bottom line.

EDDIE

You're dealing with an irrational girl. *That's* your problem.

BILLY *pushes the* GUY *away from him again.*

BILLY

Listen, find somewhere else to stand, buddy.

CELLMATE

What's wrong, cutie? Am I bothering you?

EDDIE

You heard him, back off.

The GUY *grabs at* BILLY. BILLY *pushes him off.*

CELLMATE

You going to do something about it?

He grabs at BILLY *again.*

CELLMATE

Huh?

EDDIE (*yelling*)

Back off him, schmuck!

CELLMATE (*to* BILLY)

You going to do something about it? Huh? Huh? Huh?

BILLY *pushes the* GUY *back against the wall and then goes into a boxing stance.*

> BILLY *(very calmly)*
> You want to fight? That what you want? Come on. Come on,
> you son of a bitch. I'll hit you so hard I'll kill your whole family.

BILLY *stands waiting.*

The GUY *doesn't know what to make of this threat. He could be dealing with a real tough kid. He looks at* BILLY, *unsure whether to test him.*

BILLY *stands ready.* EDDIE *watches. After a few seconds the* GUY *sits down on the cot.* BILLY *sneaks* EDDIE *a look and smiles.*

96. Interior. Police station. Night.

BILLY, EDDIE, SHREVIE, *and their* FATHERS *walk down the corridor.*

> MR. SIMMONS
> We called Timmy's father, but he said he wouldn't post bail
> until the morning. He wants to teach him a lesson.

The camera pans to BILLY *and his* FATHER.

> MR. HALPERT
> We get back from Florida, open the door, and the police call.

> BILLY
> That's what I call good timing. How's Mom?

> MR. HALPERT
> She's fine. I thought you were going to come down for a few
> days after the school break.

> BILLY
> Things came up.

They round a corner. The camera holds on the empty corridor.

Cut to

97. Interior. Diner. Night.

SHREVIE *and* MODELL *sit in a booth.*

> MODELL
> He was punching out wise men?

> SHREVIE
> Yeah, he was punching out the wise men. He was so incredibly
> drunk. I can't believe his father leaves him in jail overnight.

MODELL

He was punching out the wise men? He knocked over the whole manger?

SHREVIE

His family situation isn't the best—in between his father and his—

They're interrupted by METHAN, *who leans into their booth.*

METHAN

"And why furnish your enemies with ammunition? You're a family man, Harvey, and some day, God willing, you may want to be president, and there you are out in the open. For any hep person knows that this guy is toting this guy around with you. . . . Are we kids or what?"

SHREVIE

Will you get out of here, Methan.

METHAN

"Thanks, JJ, for what I consider sound advice."

SHREVIE

Take a walk. Would you get out of here!

METHAN *starts to walk away from the booth.*

MODELL

Is he crazy, or am I mistaken?

METHAN *walks off.*

SHREVIE

Movie freak.

98. Interior. Diner.

Angle on EDDIE *and* BOOGIE *sitting at the counter.*

EDDIE

Do you think I'm doing the right thing, getting married?

BOOGIE

Eddie, I can't tell you that.

EDDIE

I keep thinking I'm missing out on things, you know.

BOOGIE

That's what marriage is all about.

> EDDIE

I never did a lot before, you know.

> BOOGIE

What?

> EDDIE

I never did a lot of screwing around. . . . Some of course . . . a little.

> BOOGIE

A little?

> EDDIE

A little.

> BOOGIE

You son of a bitch! You're a virgin aren't ya?

> EDDIE

Technically.

> BOOGIE

Eddie, you've got a lot to learn.

> EDDIE

And am I going to learn from Elyse? Elyse doesn't know any-thing. We'll be in trouble.

Cut to

99. Interior. Beauty salon. Day.

BOOGIE *is finishing putting rollers in a middle-aged* WOMAN's *hair.*

> WOMAN

One of these days I may try another hairstyle, not yet.

> BOOGIE

Whenever you're ready.

BOOGIE *notices* BETH *enter the store. She looks around and then approaches* BOOGIE.

> BETH

Hi, Boog.

> BOOGIE (*with a hairpin in his mouth*)

Beth.

> BETH

Is Mr. Sol here?

BOOGIE

He'll be back. He went down the street for some doughnuts and coffee. What's up?

He puts the last curler in place.

BETH

Well, you know, we're all getting our hair done for the wedding.

BOOGIE *leads the* WOMAN *toward the hair driers.* BETH *follows.*

BETH (*continuing*)

The bridesmaids, the whole group. And I'm in charge of making sure that Mr. Sol can handle us. Without any problems. Maybe have extra operators or something.

BOOGIE *sits the* WOMAN *down under the drier and turns the machine on. He hands her a magazine.*

BOOGIE (*to the* WOMAN)

Here's *The Saturday Evening Post.*

(*to* BETH)

I don't know what he's planned.

BETH

You're not working that day, are you?

A stocky GUY *enters the salon.* BOOGIE *notices.*

BOOGIE

No. So I guess he's got something arranged.

The GUY *motions for* BOOGIE *to come over.*

BOOGIE (*continuing*)

He'll be back. Wait around.

BOOGIE *walks to the front of the store, where the* GUY *waits.*

BOOGIE (*continuing*)

How you doing, Tank?

TANK *nods for* BOOGIE *to follow. They exit the beauty salon.*

Cut to

100. Exterior. Beauty salon. Day.

TANK *and* BOOGIE *come out of the shop and walk around the side of the building toward a small alley.*

TANK

You had a payment to make.

BOOGIE

Yeah, I'll have it tonight.

TANK

Suppose to have it last night. No one in the office got a call.

BOOGIE

It was a mistake. Forgot. Tonight. I've got some bets that I've called in. I'll have it.

TANK *looks* BOOGIE *straight in the eye.*

TANK

Don't bullshit me, Boogie.

BOOGIE

Straight. I'll have it.

TANK *starts to turn away. He quickly turns back and punches* BOOGIE *with a hard fist to the stomach.* BOOGIE *doubles up. His breathing comes hard and fast.*

TANK

Who do you think you're fucking with? You think this is kid's stuff?

He pushes the now helpless BOOGIE *against the wall.*

TANK (*continuing*)

You think this is fun and games? Little game that kids play, huh?

He slaps BOOGIE *around the head.*

TANK (*continuing*)

'Cause, I'm not amused. Tonight, Boogie. No if, and's, or but's.

TANK *walks away.* BOOGIE *slowly straightens up, takes in a few breaths, and feels his stomach.*

Cut to

101. Interior. Beauty salon. Minutes later.

BOOGIE *enters the shop.*

BEAUTICIAN

Boogie, there's a call for you.

BOOGIE *has got himself together. He walks to the phone and answers it.*

BOOGIE

Hello? . . . Carol? . . . Just thinking about you. . . . What?
. . . The flu? Are you sure? . . . One hundred two, yeah, that
doesn't sound good. . . . OK, babe. Take care. I'll call and check
up on you. . . . Feel better. . . . Bye.

BOOGIE *hangs up the phone and leans back against the wall. He's in deep trouble. He looks
across the room at* BETH, *who sits in a chair reading a magazine. He watches her. Thoughts
race across his mind. He walks over to her and sits down.*

BOOGIE (*continuing*)

Feeling better today?

BETH

I'm not crying. That's about the only improvement. Thanks for
last night. I needed someone to just be there.

BOOGIE

Felt like old times, you know. Standing in the doorway.

(*a small laugh*)

Like I was dating you again.

BETH

Boog, when we were dating, did you care for me?

BOOGIE

Sure I did.

BETH

Not because you could do things to me, but because you cared?

BOOGIE

Of course, Beth. There were plenty of girls for that, you know,
if a guy wanted a pop. But I got to tell you, you were real good.

BETH

I was?

BOOGIE

Believe me.

BETH

How would I rate?

BOOGIE

Right up there. We had some good nights. Still think about
those times, and that's long ago.

BETH *looks away. Her eyes start to tear. She is on the edge of breaking down.*

                  BETH

I don't have any sense what I'm like anymore. Don't know what
I am. If what I wear is nice . . . If I look pretty . . . Just lost all
sense of me.

                 BOOGIE

I don't know what Shrevie doesn't tell ya, but you have nothing
to worry about. You're a definite looker. A sexy lady.

                (a beat)

We should get together sometime.

They sit in the chairs, looking off in opposite directions.

          BOOGIE *(continuing)*

Shrevie going over to Eddie's for Elyse's football test?

                 BETH

Yeah? Are you going?

                 BOOGIE

No.

                 BETH

Can we get together tonight, Boog?

BOOGIE *has accomplished what he wants, but he's not happy about it.*

                 BOOGIE

Yes.

Cut to

102. Interior. Television-station corridor. Night.

BILLY *and* BARBARA *walk down the corridor.* BILLY *is angry.*

                 BILLY

It's mine as well. I have something to say in this as well. Don't
I?

        BARBARA *(speaking quietly)*

I'm not talking about doing anything drastic, an abortion or
anything like that.

                 BILLY

Well, I get the feeling I'm not even included.

             BARBARA

Keep your voice down.

BILLY

I'm half-responsible for this mess!

BARBARA

Please. Don't be so loud.

She sees a door and opens it.

BARBARA (*continuing*)

In here.

BILLY *enters. She closes the door behind them.*

Cut to

103. Interior. Television news-announcer's booth.

Through the glass partition we see the control room and the studio floor below. There is some activity going on in preparation for the midday newscast.

BILLY

Have you been to the doctor yet?

BARBARA

No.

BILLY

Why not?

BARBARA

I'm afraid to. Confirm your worst fears, as they say.

Cut to

104. Interior. Television-station control room.

A TECHNICIAN *is checking out equipment prior to air time. In the background, through the glass partition, we see* BARBARA *and* BILLY *talking in the announcer's booth.*

On the monitors above we see the daily soap operas. The audio of one of them is on. The AUDIO MAN *asks for voice checks on the floor microphones.*

Cut back to

105. Interior. Television news-announcer's booth.

BILLY

What do we do? Don't you think we should explore the situation?

BARBARA *sits on the desk. A small light is directly behind her. It is not on.*

> BARBARA
>
> I can't believe this happened. I'm hardly the adventurous type. Somehow it just doesn't seem fair.

Cut back to

106. Interior. Television-station control room.

The AUDIO MAN *completes his check. Directly behind him we see* BILLY *and* BARBARA *in the glass booth.* BILLY *picks up a paper and puts his feet up on the audio console. Accidently he kicks on a switch.*

Cut back to

107. Interior. Television news-announcer's room.

The light behind BARBARA *turns red.*

> BARBARA
>
> And that makes it very difficult.

Cut back to

108. Interior. Television-station control room.

The soap opera continues. We hear the audio of the show. A COUPLE *is having lunch in a restaurant.*

We also hear BILLY *and* BARBARA*'s voices coming through, but very low key.*

> SOAP OPERA MAN
>
> I think it's important, and sometimes I feel that we've neglected to discuss it.

> SOAP OPERA WOMAN
>
> Are you saying that it's my fault?

> SOAP OPERA MAN
>
> No, no . . . of course not. It's no one's fault. But I only mentioned this because if you let time pass, the problems compound themselves. And that would be unfortunate for both of us.

> SOAP OPERA WOMAN
>
> Would it be better if we just let time pass?

> SOAP OPERA MAN
>
> He's very, very ill.

SOAP OPERA WOMAN

You were there?

BARBARA'S VOICE

I have a great affection for you, Willy. You're my closest friend.

SOAP OPERA WOMAN

If he dies, what will we do?

The camera holds on the soap opera monitors, the AUDIO MAN, *who is reading the paper, and* BILLY *and* BARBARA *in the background.*

BARBARA'S VOICE

I won't marry you, not out of convenience.

SOAP OPERA MAN

I think we should wait.

BARBARA'S VOICE

Not because it's the thing to do. God, I sound disgustingly brave.

SOAP OPERA WOMAN

It's not going to be easy when I talk to Terry.

SOAP OPERA MAN

Is it necessary that you talk to him?

SOAP OPERA WOMAN

What do *you* suggest?

SOAP OPERA MAN

I'm not sure, but I don't . . . I don't know.

SOAP OPERA WOMAN

Margaret did. She made the break. There were no hard feelings.

SOAP OPERA MAN

Well, good for Margaret, but that doesn't really pertain to us, does it?

SOAP OPERA WOMAN

I'm just trying to find an answer.

SOAP OPERA MAN

Something else to drink?

SOAP OPERA WOMAN

No . . .

Cut to

109. Interior. Simmons' basement. Night.

We are looking up a flight of steps. A door opens. MR. SIMMONS *stands there.*

MR. SIMMONS (*yelling down*)

How's she doing?

SHREVIE (*offscreen*)

Elyse has about a seventy-two so far, but she's hitting a bad streak.

EDDIE'S FATHER *comes down the steps. We see* SHREVIE, FENWICK, MODELL, *and* BILLY *gathered. The basement has a bar with neon lights around it, so as to set it off as a showpiece in the room. The walls are knotty pine.* EDDIE *and* ELYSE *are not in the room. They are in the laundry room. The door is partially open.*

EDDIE (*offscreen*)

Before the Cleveland Browns joined the NFL they were in another league. What was it called?

ELYSE (*offscreen*)

Another league?

EDDIE (*offscreen*)

Yes.

A long pause—the GUYS *eagerly await the answer.*

ELYSE (*offscreen*)

I don't know.

SHREVIE *shakes his head and makes a mark on a piece of paper.*

BILLY

What's it now?

SHREVIE

I don't know anymore. Maybe about a sixty-seven.

BILLY

Passing is sixty-five?

SHREVIE

Yep.

EDDIE (*offscreen*)

Buddy Young played for a team that no longer exists. What was the name of that team?

All the GUYS *look at one another. A very tough question.*

MR. SIMMONS
Anybody know that?

None of the GUYS *has the faintest idea.*

ELYSE (*offscreen*)
The New York Yankees football team.

EDDIE (*offscreen*)
Right.

MODELL
The New York Yankees football team?

MR. SIMMONS
They were also in the American Conference. I contributed that question.

EDDIE (*offscreen*)
What was the longest run from scrimmage by a rookie in his first game?

SHREVIE
Alan Ameche.

EDDIE (*offscreen*)
We heard that in here. I'm disqualifying that question.

ELYSE (*offscreen*)
I knew that. Seventy-nine yard run. Opening day 1955.

EDDIE (*offscreen*)
Sorry, Elyse.

BILLY
You blew that, Shrevie.

SHREVIE
Sorry. I got excited. It's one of the few questions I knew.

BILLY
How many more?

SHREVIE
I don't know. I've lost count.

The door to the top of the stairs opens. MRS. SIMMONS *stands there.*

MRS. SIMMONS
Elyse's mother is on the phone. How's she doing?

MR. SIMMONS
The guys think it could go either way.

MRS. SIMMONS

Either way. OK.

She closes the door.

EDDIE (*offscreen*)

The Colts signed him. A Heisman trophy winner who decided
to play in Canada. Now, however, he plays for the team. What's
his name.

The camera pans the faces of the GUYS.

ELYSE (*offscreen*)

Heisman trophy winner. L. G. Dupre.

EDDIE (*offscreen*)

No. Billy Vessels.

ELYSE (*offscreen*)

I should have known that.

EDDIE (*offscreen*)

Should of's don't count.

FENWICK

Vessels. Out of Oklahoma.

MODELL

She could of racked up points on that one.

SHREVIE

I have no idea what the score is now.

MODELL

Want to bet she goes down for the count?

EDDIE (*offscreen*)

Last question.

The GUYS *and* MR. SIMMONS *tighten up. Tension fills the room.*

EDDIE (*offscreen, continuing*)

The Colts had a team here, lost the franchise, then got one from
Dallas. What were the colors of the original Colt team?

FENWICK

Woo. A ball buster.

MODELL (*mumbling to himself*)

The original colors?

MR. SIMMONS

Also my question.

ELYSE (*offscreen*)
Original colors? Green and gray.

EDDIE (*offscreen*)
Right.

BILLY (*jumping up and applauding*)
A real scrapper! Tough question and she pulls it out of a hat.

The other GUYS *don't share his excitement.*

BILLY (*continuing*)
Come on, guys. Green and gray. Any of you guys know that?
Come on. Give her credit.

We hear EDDIE's *voice. The* GUYS *quickly shush* BILLY.

SHREVIE
Total's coming up.

EDDIE (*offscreen*)
True and false—seventy-two. Multiple choice—fifty-eight.

MODELL
Killer choices. Confusing.

EDDIE (*offscreen*)
Short answer—sixty-four.

EDDIE *totals. The* GUYS *wait.*

BILLY
What do you think?

MODELL
Pick 'em.

MR. SIMMONS *walks to the bar and pours a drink.*

EDDIE (*offscreen*)
The total is . . . sixty-three.

ELYSE (*offscreen*)
Oh no!

FENWICK
A cliff-hanger.

BILLY
Two points.

SHREVIE
What do you think he'll do?

MR. SIMMONS

He'll give it to her. Good sportsmanship is worth two points.

The door to the laundry room opens. EDDIE *steps into the room. He looks at the* GUYS *and his* FATHER.

EDDIE

The marriage is off.

Cut to

110. Interior. Boogie's car. Night.

He sits in the car and waits. BETH *comes out of the house and down the walk. She gets into the car and slams the door shut. She is excited. She leans over and kisses* BOOGIE *on the cheek.*

BETH

Where are we going?

BOOGIE

Fenwick's apartment.

He hands her a long, blond wig.

BOOGIE *(continuing)*

Here, put this on.

BETH

What's that for?

BOOGIE

Case someone sees us. They might think you're Carol Hea-throw or somebody like that.

She slips the wig on and straightens it out.

BETH

How's it look?

BOOGIE

Fine. Just fine.

They drive away.

Cut to

111. Exterior. Simmons' house. Night.

FENWICK *and* SHREVIE *walk out the front door. From inside we hear yelling and screaming between* EDDIE *and his* PARENTS.

SHREVIE
You going up to the diner?

FENWICK
No, got to validate the Heathrow bet.

SHREVIE
Christ, yeah, of course.

They approach their cars.

SHREVIE *(continuing)*
Fen, you mind if I come along?

FENWICK *thinks about it.*

SHREVIE *(continuing)*
I won't make a sound.

FENWICK
It's a small closet. Gotta be still.

SHREVIE
Great.

They get into FENWICK's *car and drive off.*
Cut to

112. Exterior. Street. Night.

BOOGIE *drives his DeSoto along.* BETH, *wearing the blond wig, sits by his side.*
Cut to

113. Exterior. Street. Night.

FENWICK's *Triumph turns a corner and heads down another street.*
Cut to

114. Interior. Fenwick's car. Night.

FENWICK
"My Prayer"?

SHREVIE
Flip side—"Heaven on Earth"—recorded by The Platters for
Mercury Records. Color of label—maroon.

FENWICK

"I'm Stickin' with You"?

SHREVIE

"I'm Stickin' with You"? Flip side is "Ever Lovin' Fingers"
recorded by Jimmy Bowen for Roulette Records. Color of label
is orange.

FENWICK

"Donna"?

SHREVIE

Flip side . . .

FENWICK

I thought that was the flip side.

SHREVIE

It's "La Bamba."

FENWICK *sings "La Bamba."*

115. Interior. Boogie's car. Night.

BOOGIE *is uncomfortable, knowing what he is about to do is wrong.* BETH *is silent.*

Cut to

116. Interior. Fenwick's apartment. Night.

FENWICK *and* SHREVIE *enter the dark apartment.* FENWICK *doesn't turn on the lights. They
move toward the bedroom.*

Cut to

117. Interior. Fenwick's bedroom.

The room is dark. A shaft of light coming through a window offers the only illumination.
FENWICK *opens the closet door.* SHREVIE *steps inside.*

FENWICK

You crouch. I'll stand.

SHREVIE *kneels down.* FENWICK *enters and closes the door. It remains about four inches open.*

Cut to

118. Interior. Fenwick's closet.

The GUYS' *point of view—part of the room and the bed*

> FENWICK (*offscreen*)
> Yeah, this'll be fine.

> SHREVIE (*offscreen*)
> Fine with me. Good view.

Cut to

119. Exterior. Fenwick's apartment. Night.

BOOGIE *and* BETH *are walking toward the apartment building.*

> BOOGIE
> You've got to be real quiet inside. No talking.

> BETH
> I think you're a little paranoid.

> BOOGIE
> The walls are very, very thin. Promise?

> BETH
> Sure.

They approach the door. BOOGIE *unlocks it. He starts to open the door, then closes it. He's changed his mind.*

> BOOGIE
> Let's go.

He takes her by the arm and leads her away. BETH *is confused.*

> BOOGIE (*continuing*)
> It's a mistake, Beth. Bet or no bet.

> BETH
> What?

They approach the car. BOOGIE *opens the door.* BETH *gets inside.*

> BETH (*continuing*)
> What are you talking about?

BOOGIE *closes the door and goes around to his side. He gets in, starts the engine, and pulls away.*

Cut to

120. Interior. Fenwick's bedroom.

Angle on the slightly opened closet door

> FENWICK (*offscreen*)
>
> They should be here now.

> SHREVIE (*offscreen*)
>
> Let's wait.

Cut to

121. Interior. Boogie's car.

BOOGIE *is very upset with himself.* BETH *is calm. She holds the blond wig in her lap.*

> BETH
>
> I was suppose to be Carol Heathrow?

> BOOGIE
>
> That's right. Sick thing to do. I'm real sorry.

They drive in silence. BETH *plays with the strands of hair on the wig.*

> BETH
>
> Thank you.

> BOOGIE
>
> For what?

> BETH
>
> At least you had enough respect for me to call it off. That says a lot.

> BOOGIE (*a beat*)
>
> Shrevie and you should work out your thing.

> BETH
>
> I wish I knew what to do.

> BOOGIE
>
> I'm not real good at talking to girls when there's problems and all. With me, if I have a hassle with a girl, I just split. But you guys should try something. It would be worth it.

> BETH
>
> Boog, when I came into the beauty parlor this morning, were you lying?

BOOGIE
You'll always rate right up there.

Cut to

•

122. Exterior. Shrevie and Beth's house. Night.

BOOGIE's *car is pulled over.* BETH's *door is open, and she stands on the curb talking to* BOOGIE *inside the car.*

BETH
What are you going to do about the money?

BOOGIE *shrugs his shoulders and smiles at her.*

BOOGIE
I don't know.

BETH *closes the door.* BOOGIE *drives away.* BETH *watches as he disappears down the street.*

Cut to

123. Interior. Fenwick's bedroom.

Angle on slightly opened closet door. FENWICK *and* SHREVIE *are still in the closet.*

FENWICK
Come on, Boogie.

SHREVIE
I bet he's getting her in the hallway.

124. Interior. Strip joint. Night.

BILLY *and* EDDIE *are in one of the clubs on Baltimore's famous Block. In the background a bored* STRIPPER *goes through the motions. The* DRUMMER *thumps out a monotonous beat and a* SAXOPHONIST *drones away. A few* SAILORS *and some other* CUSTOMERS *sit at tables around the stage. All the tables have wooden mallets. When the* STRIPPER *does something they especially like, the* CUSTOMERS *pound the table with the mallet.*

BILLY *and* EDDIE *both have beers and chasers in front of them.* BILLY *sips the chaser, and his body actually shakes from it for a few seconds.*

BILLY
There is no reason to actually like this; you know that.

EDDIE
An acquired taste.

BILLY

No matter how long I drink whiskey, I still don't like it.

He takes another sip and once again shakes. Then he sips the beer.

BILLY *(continuing)*

Now beer's another story.

EDDIE *watches the* STRIPPER *throwing a few bumps and grinds.*

EDDIE

You know something?

BILLY

What?

EDDIE

I don't like strippers. I mean, so they show a little here and there. So what? But give me a couple of mamoosas in a pink sweater . . . look out!

BILLY

Remember the first time we became aware of breasts on girls?

EDDIE

Arlene Stowe.

BILLY

Showed up for the new school year, and there they were.

EDDIE

Seventh grade. We gave little Joel Barry a nickel apiece to find out if they were real. Told him to be subtle. He walked over, reached up, and grabbed. Turned to us and yelled, "They're real!"

BILLY

The whole thing with girls is painful. And it keeps getting more painful . . . instead of easier.

BILLY *downs his beer and orders two more.*

EDDIE

Remember copping a feel? Boogie was the first. Said it was great. So when I took out Ruth Ray I figured I had to do it.

BILLY

Ruth Ray, eighth grade.

EDDIE

Right. Sat on the couch in her club cellar for hours trying to

figure out a way to get my arm around her. Finally I learned the
move. I yawned and put my arm around her shoulder.

He demonstrates on BILLY.

> EDDIE (*continuing*)
> Then came the big task of getting my hand down to her breast.
> By the time I worked up the nerve to move down, I realized my
> arm was asleep. Figured out there wasn't enough time to take
> it back, get the feeling again, and start over. Had to be in by
> eleven. Time was running out. So I move toward the breast with
> my arm asleep. My first copping a feel was like this.

He bangs his limp arm against BILLY's *chest. He bumps it again.*

> EDDIE (*continuing*)
> Next time I saw the guys they said, "Did you cop a feel?" I said
> "Yeah." "How was it?" "Great."

> BILLY
> Now wait a second. You mean you never copped a feel for Ruth
> Ray?

> EDDIE
> You believed me.

They laugh.

Cut to

125. Exterior. Diner. Night.

BOOGIE *pulls into the diner parking lot.* FENWICK *and* SHREVIE *are there already, sitting in the Triumph.*

> FENWICK
> Hey, Boogie's here.
>
> (*yelling over to* BOOGIE)
> Hey, Boog, . . . where were you tonight, Mr. Boog?

> SHREVIE
> You chicken out?

> BOOGIE
> Yeah, I chickened out.

> FENWICK
> Boog, you should get outta here. Tank's inside.

BOOGIE *gets out of the car and slams the door shut. He looks toward the diner and thinks for a moment.*

SHREVIE

Why don't you wait until he splits?

BOOGIE

He'll just keep looking for me.

He starts toward the diner.

BOOGIE (*continuing*)

Hand's dealt. Might as well play the cards.

The GUYS *hang behind.* BOOGIE *continues on. Inside the diner we see* TANK *moving along the aisle toward the door. He comes outside.*

TANK

Boog.

BOOGIE

Tank.

TANK

Lucky man.

BOOGIE

That so.

TANK

Yeah. The Bagel just paid off your debt.

BOOGIE *looks at him, trying to size up the situation, wondering if he's running a number for some reason.*

BOOGIE

We're even? Straight?

TANK

That's the story.

TANK *starts past* BOOGIE.

BOOGIE

Tank!

TANK *turns.* BOOGIE *slams his fist into his stomach.* TANK *drops to one knee in pain. In the background we hear* SHREVIE *and* FENWICK *whooping and hollering.*

SHREVIE (*offscreen*)

He put him down! He put him down! Go Boogie.

FENWICK (*offscreen*)

Definitely the smile of the week.

BOOGIE (*to* TANK)

I still owed you that.

He enters the diner with SHREVIE *and* FENWICK *still yelling their approval.*
Cut to

126. Interior. Diner. Night.

BOOGIE *approaches* BAGEL, *who sits at a booth alone. He joins him.*

BOOGIE

Thanks, Bagel.

BAGEL

Your mother called. She was frantic. So out of respect for your
father . . .

He sips his coffee. Then he picks up a toasted bagel and butters it.

BAGEL (*continuing*)

Your mother feels you're just wasting your time in law school.
. . . It's not for you.

BOOGIE

Probably right.

BAGEL

Come to work for me. There's a lot of money to be made in the
home-improvement business. You'd be very good at it.

BOOGIE *thinks about it.* BAGEL *chews on his bagel.*

BOOGIE

Well, I was only really using law as a come-on for the girls.
They like that. But, what the hell.

(*smiling*)

I can always lie.

The WAITRESS *passes.*

BOOGIE (*continuing*)

Enid, some french fries and gravy.

BAGEL

Call the two thousand an advance.

BOOGIE

I'll work for you . . . for a while. Then I'll have to move on to
bigger things.

BAGEL
Always a dreamer, eh Boog?

BOOGIE
If you don't have good dreams, Bagel, you've got nightmares.

He flashes him a smile.

Cut to

127. Interior. Strip joint. Night.

BILLY *and* EDDIE *are still drinking at the bar. They are not drunk, just very happy.*

EDDIE
I'll tell you one thing that happens when you get married. You have to give up your old friends.

BILLY *listens to the music, slapping his thighs, trying to get the band to pick up the beat.*

EDDIE *(continuing)*
The wife wants you to get new friends. 'Cause me and you have secrets she'll never know. And new friends can never be as good, 'cause we've got a history.

BILLY
It won't change, only if we let it.

BILLY *keeps slapping his thighs, but the* DRUMMER *and the* SAXOPHONIST *continue on, unaware of* BILLY's *private urgings.*

BILLY *(continuing)*
This is getting me crazy.

BILLY *goes toward the small stage.*

BILLY *(offscreen continuing)*
Come on, guys! Pick up the beat!

They don't respond. EDDIE *sits at the bar amused.* BILLY *claps his hands to a strong rhythm, but of course the* GUYS *pay no attention.*

BILLY *goes up on the stage and pulls a cover off a small piano in the corner. He sits down, runs his fingers down the keyboard, then starts to play. It has a nice, pleasant sound to it. The* DRUMMER *and the* SAXOPHONIST *stop, not knowing what to do. The* STRIPPER *also stops.*

The club BOUNCER *at the front door turns toward the stage, notices something is wrong, and makes his way forward.*

BILLY's *piano playing becomes more intense. He drives the keys hard—full-tilt rock and roll. The sound becomes infectious. The* SAILORS *and other* CUSTOMERS *pick up the beat. One after another they start to pound the table with the wooden mallets.*

EDDIE *moves toward the stage banging empty beer bottles together.*

The SAXOPHONIST *joins* BILLY. *Then the* DRUMMER. *The* STRIPPER *stands by the side of the stage watching. The music builds.*

BILLY's *fingers pound the piano.* EDDIE *jumps up on the stage and starts dancing around. He grabs the* STRIPPER, *and they jitterbug.*

The SAILORS *and other* CUSTOMERS *are on their feet, banging the mallets on the tables for all they are worth—a room full of drummers. The tempo heightens.*

BILLY *kicks back the stool à la Jerry Lee Lewis. The* CROWD *cheers. The* BOUNCER *cheers along.*

The SAXOPHONIST *struts the stage playing his heart out. The* DRUMMER *drives the bass drum with his foot. His hands sweep back and forth across the skins.*

EDDIE's *feet are flying—enthusiasm over grace. The* STRIPPER *is a whirlwind of motion and sexuality. The tempo is fierce.*

BILLY *gives a look to the* DRUMMER *and the* SAXOPHONIST. *The music builds and builds, and then altogether they shut down. The place explodes in cheers and applause.*

Cut to

128. Exterior. The Block. Night.

BILLY *and* EDDIE *walk with their arms around the* STRIPPER. *They are enjoying one another.*

EDDIE

Let's see.

STRIPPER

First joke you remember.

EDDIE

Ah, let's see. Fifth grade. *Junior Scholastic Magazine.* "Hickory dickory dock. The mouse ran up the clock. The clock struck one . . . and the other two escaped with minor injuries."

BILLY *and the* STRIPPER *boo.* EDDIE *laughs.*

STRIPPER

That's terrible.

EDDIE

Fifth-grade humor.

STRIPPER

Since then your humor has moved up to the sixth grade, is that it?

EDDIE *laughs. He enjoys the put-down.*

EDDIE

You're all right.

STRIPPER

You guys have made my night. You should come down and hang out more often.

EDDIE

Don't think I can. Getting married.

BILLY *looks at him.* EDDIE *smiles.*

EDDIE (*continuing, to* BILLY)

Figured she would have gotten the Alan Ameche question that Shrevie screwed up.

BILLY

Benefit of the doubt.

EDDIE

Exactly.

STRIPPER

I love weddings. Just never found the time to settle . . . or wanted to.

(*to* BILLY)

And you?

BILLY

No marriage.

STRIPPER

Got a girl?

BILLY

Not really. Just in love.

STRIPPER

Does the girl know?

BILLY

Yeah, I told her about it.

STRIPPER

Told her? Did you show her?

BILLY *thinks about that as they enter an all-night coffee shop.*

Cut to

129. Exterior. Coffee shop. Dawn.

BILLY, EDDIE, *and the* STRIPPER *sit in a booth by the window, eating, drinking, and laughing.*

The camera slowly pulls back. The first rays of morning light are breaking behind the building. The camera keeps pulling back.

Cut to

130. Exterior. Countryside. Day.

JANE CHISOLM *rides her horse across the gently rolling hills.*

The horse and she are as one—grace and beauty. She rides out of the frame. Seconds later BOOGIE *rides a horse into the frame. He pulls up on the horse and comes to a stop. He watches* JANE *ride, then pulls up the collar on his wool overcoat and rides off.*

BOOGIE *rides after* JANE. *Although he is not a good rider, he pushes to pick up ground. Finally he pulls alongside.*

JANE *slows her horse, and* BOOGIE *does the same with his.*

> BOOGIE
>
> Nice morning.

> JANE
>
> Yes, it is.

> BOOGIE
>
> Mornings I've always felt are a good time to ride.

JANE *doesn't respond.*

> BOOGIE (*continuing*)
>
> You live around here?

> JANE
>
> Not around here. Here.

BOOGIE *looks around what seems like endless countryside. He's overwhelmed.*

> JANE (*continuing*)
>
> Which means you are trespassing.

BOOGIE *looks her in the eye and flashes his smile.*

BOOGIE

I was waiting for an invite.

JANE *studies him.*

JANE

Let's ride.

She kicks her horse and gallops off.

BOOGIE *follows. They ride away from the camera.*

JANE (*continuing*)

What's your name?

BOOGIE

Boogie. As in Bobby Sheftel.

They ride over a crest and disappear from sight.

Cut to

131. Interior. Banquet-hall Wedding Room. Night.

The Wedding Room has been elaborately decorated. Potted blue and white flowers in stands line the aisle to the blue and white flowered altar. The room is a festival of blue and white.

The GUESTS sit in folding chairs eagerly waiting for the wedding procession to begin.

The music begins. It is not the traditional wedding march but rather the Baltimore Colts fight song. Even though the organist has softened it, there is still a rah-rah quality to it. The FLOWER GIRL comes down the aisle throwing white flowers onto the blue aisle.

MODELL'S GIRLFRIEND

What is that music?

MODELL

Colt marching song. Sounds good, huh? Very tasteful.

The USHERS come forward—BOOGIE and FENWICK, followed by SHREVIE, who walks alone. They are all smartly dressed in black tuxedos.

The BRIDESMAIDS come forward—BETH and another GIRL, followed by two more GIRLS, followed by two more GIRLS.

BILLY and EDDIE start down the aisle. Behind them are MR. and MRS. SIMMONS. They walk on either side of EDDIE's GRANDMOTHER.

The Colts fight song continues.

EDDIE sees someone sitting one seat in from the aisle. He whispers to BILLY.

BILLY

Moon Shaw? Where?

EDDIE indicates with a nod. BILLY looks over.

BILLY *(continuing)*

You're right?

As they start to pass, BILLY leans into the row and grabs MOON SHAW by the shirt. He pulls back his fist. MOON is shocked.

BILLY *(continuing)*

Hi, Moon.

He smiles, lets him go, and rejoins EDDIE, having missed only a few steps. No one is quite sure what has happened. Quickly the attention is back on the wedding procession.

132. Interior. Banquet-hall Wedding Room.

Long shot—the hall—as ELYSE and her MOTHER and FATHER come down the aisle. Cut to

133. Interior. Banquet-hall Wedding Room.

Tight shot—EDDIE's face

RABBI *(offscreen)*

Do you, Edward, take this woman, Elyse, to be your lawful wedded wife? For better or worse, in sickness and in health, until death do you part?

EDDIE

I do.

RABBI *(offscreen)*

Do you, Elyse . . .

134. Interior. Banquet-hall Wedding Room.

Tight shot—FENWICK's face

RABBI *(offscreen)*

take this man, Edward, to be . . .

135. Interior. Banquet-hall Wedding Room.

Tight shot—BOOGIE's face

> RABBI (*offscreen*)
> your lawful wedded husband. For better or worse, . . .

136. Interior. Banquet-hall Wedding Room.

Tight shot—BILLY's face

> RABBI (*offscreen*)
> in sickness and in health, till death do you part?

137. Interior. Banquet-hall Wedding Room.

Tight shot—EDDIE's face

> ELYSE (*offscreen*)
> I do.

EDDIE *smiles.*

> RABBI (*offscreen*)
> I now pronounce you man and wife.

Cut to

138. Interior. Banquet hall.

The hall is also decorated in blue and white—the tablecloths, napkins, ribbons, flowers, the bandstand, the band.

The six-piece BAND plays a nice, perky, dance tune. Some WOMEN dance with WOMEN. MOTHERS dance with SONS, FATHERS with DAUGHTERS, and some HUSBANDS with WIVES.

The camera pans to a banner on the back wall. It reads EDDIE AND ELYSE—FOR THE 60S AND FOREVER.

SHREVIE dances with BETH, and they seem to be enjoying themselves. BETH is counting the steps to the dance for SHREVIE.

> BETH
> One, two, three. . . . One, two, three. . . .

> SHREVIE
> You look very pretty. Blue becomes you.
>
> (*a beat*)
> I've made us some reservations for the summer in the Poconos.

BETH

How long?

SHREVIE

I think we might go for ten days.

BETH

Ten days is good.

The camera pans to FENWICK *and the eleventh-grader,* DIANE.

FENWICK

I'm thinking of going to Europe.

DIANE

Why not travel the United States?

FENWICK

It's been done. Europe. Europe looks like a smile.

The camera pans to EDDIE *dancing with his* MOTHER.

EDDIE

It's not like I'm going to another country.

MRS. SIMMONS

Please come back soon. . . . I'll make you sandwiches.

139. Interior. Banquet hall.

Angle on SINGER *on stage. He is singing "Blue Moon."*

The camera pans to BOOGIE *and* JANE CHISOLM *sitting at a table.*

BOOGIE

Can I get you something?

JANE

Bobby, I think I will have a few more of . . .

(*holding up an hors d'oeuvre*)

whatever these are.

Cut to

140. Interior. Banquet hall. Slightly later.

A slow song is playing. BILLY *and* BARBARA *dance.*

BARBARA

I made arrangements with my boss. He said not to worry. The
job was mine.

BILLY

That was nice of him.

BARBARA

So I'll work and care for the child. It can be done. I'll just have to put up with those who want to think badly of me.

BILLY

That's not going to be easy.

BARBARA

I know.

They move across the floor. BILLY *holds her close.*

BARBARA (*continuing*)

The baby is ours, Willy. We can both celebrate that. You can love him just as much, spend time with him or her.

BOOGIE *and* JANE *pass them.* BOOGIE *kisses* JANE *lightly on the cheek.*

BILLY

You know what I realized just yesterday? I've been intimidated by you. I always liked you because you were strong, independent, and all. But I've been intimidated by that as well. I've always held back with you. When we kissed, I held back. The same when we made love in New York. I keep thinking I have to be special, like normal passion wasn't proper . . . as if it were just too ordinary and we were beyond that.

BARBARA *pulls away from him slightly so she can see his face. There's a sad look in his eyes.*

BARBARA

If that's the case, I wouldn't think that's a hard thing to correct.

She kisses him; they hold each other tightly.

BARBARA (*continuing*)

We've got plenty of time to find out about one another. Plenty of time.

He kisses her. They stand still on the dance floor as others dance around them.

Cut to

141. Interior. Banquet hall later.

MODELL *gets up onto the stage and takes the microphone.*

MODELL

I don't want to bother you; I just wanted to say a few words.
The guys wanted me to. . . . I didn't prepare anything. The guys
told me to come up and say a few words. I was thinking that
now Eddie's getting married, he won't really be hanging out
with the guys anymore; I just wanted to say we were never
really crazy about you. I'll be quite honest. I didn't want to tell
you sooner because you're a sensitive person. I just wanted to
thank everybody who's responsible for you being here, Elyse.
I don't know if everybody knows what Elyse had to go through
to get married. . . . She was just two points away from spending
the rest of her life by herself. Now she knows more about
football than most girls in America. It's important; it really is.
We all know that most marriages rely on a firm grasp of football
trivia. Eddie gets crazy sometimes with sports; I don't know
whether you know.

During this dialogue the camera pans the faces of BILLY, EDDIE, SHREVIE, FENWICK, *and*
BOOGIE *as they sit at a table together. As the dialogue continues,* ELYSE *stands with her
back to the camera, holding the bouquet up toward the eagerly waiting crowd of* GIRL-
FRIENDS. *She tosses the bouquet.*

MODELL (*offscreen, continuing*)

It's one thing to dress the room blue and white with banners,
and the cake in the shape of a football. . . . But personally I
thought it was out of line when Eddie asked the rabbi to wear
black and white stripes and a whistle.

*Everyone laughs as we see the bouquet bouncing off several extended arms before it settles
on the table where the* GUYS *are sitting. They look down at the bouquet, then up at the
camera. There is a faint smile on their faces. Freeze frame.*

The still turns to black and white.

Fade out.